Praise for *The Ghost of Rabbie Burns*

"This collection of well-crafted poems by Laurence Overmire was inspired by his pilgrimage, in 2014, to the 'enchanted land' of his forefathers, Scotland. The poet's 'yearning to connect' with his Scottish heritage is touchingly sincere and thoughtful. Many of the poems are historically informative and well researched, some atmospherically descriptive and others laced with a wry but kindly humour. The author's philosophical observations and ideals are in line with Scotland's egalitarian stance in the world often represented through the writings of Robert Burns to whom Overmire pays homage.

I have thoroughly enjoyed this poetic journey and am always gratified by the tremendous enthusiasm, joy and love displayed by the great Scottish diaspora for the culture, scenery and people of it's Motherland. This fine collection of poems from the pen of Laurence Overmire leaves us in no doubt of his sense of belonging to Scotland."

Isla St Clair, *singer and broadcaster*

"To most people there comes a time when they ask, Where do I come from? Who were my forefathers? And above all, Where do I fit in to all of this? This book, *The Ghost of Rabbie Burns*, offers the reader a pathway into the past where one can gain a true perspective of their own Scottish heritage, and for the non-Scot, an understanding of the culture with which Robert Burns wrote, and was so passionate about.

Historically interesting and accurate, intelligently put together, an ideal platform for the enquiring mind to gain a passionate perspective of olden Caledonia. Read and enjoy."

Steve McDonald, *composer, Sons of Somerled*

"Laurence has created what I would describe as a free form guide book to his ancestral home, an amusing, heartfelt, historical journey that every exile should take–in each passing generation, grows a greater patriotism for the motherland. Weel duin, Laurence."

Iain H Scott, *Scocha*

"Insightful and delightful. Overmire's account of visiting Scotland, the world of his ancestors, is heartfelt and combines history lessons with scenes as a tourist just fumbling along. *The Ghost of Rabbie Burns* reveals how a poet can connect the dots of the past and the present to the future as a visitor in the auld world."

Stewart MacNeil, *The Barra MacNeils*

"A wonderful book of poetry and a great asset if you are making a trip to Scotland."

Duke of Argyll, *Chief of Clan Campbell*

"*The Ghost of Rabbie Burns* is an engaging meditation on Scotland, its history, places and people which have contributed toward the creation of Scottish identity."

Rev. Calum I. MacLeod, *Minister of St. Giles' Cathedral, Edinburgh*

"*In here there's honest poetry,*
That paints a heart, an' a' that,
The Laurence way, through pass and glen,
We see a land an' a' that.
For a' that, an' a' that,
The map's obscure, an' a' that,
But the heart and lore comes shining through,
The book's the gowd for a' that!"
With apologies to the Bard.

The Rev Richard Frazer, *Minister of Greyfriars Kirk, Edinburgh*

"Much has been written on Robert Burns and Scotland and it is a testimony to his brilliant legacy in original works and collected songs and airs that 220 years after his death his works are still in print and in demand worldwide and translated into 22 languages.

Much of his collected works were captured during his tours of Scotland …and this book captures the mood very well as a trail through Scotland."

Jock Meikle, *President of the Burns Club of London*

"In the year 2014, Laurence Overmire and his wife embarked upon a gratifying journey to and through the Scotland of his ancestral heritage. His poetic heart is amply displayed in this collection of his efforts. His genealogical penchant for research shows itself in references within his poetry. It's a pleasant book to curl up with on a cold winter's evening in front of the fireplace, or at the beach on a sunny summer day."

Margaret Frost, *Chairman, Scottish American Society, President, American Clan Cumming Association*

"The imagery evoked in his verse and the moral lessons imparted by Laurence represent the message of Robert Burns for the modern time. We are reminded of the timelessness of the Bard and the debt we owe to improve life around us."

Mark Myers, *President, Clan Maclean Association of California, USA*

"Upon reading thru this exquisite book, I couldn't help but think of my travels thru the homeland of my forefathers. My family and I have made several excursions traveling the backroads and main highways of Alba, and continue to be left speechless in its beauty and history. When reading the book, I couldn't help but find my memories being awakened from the creativity of the author and his ability to recreate experiences I fell in love with. The art of painting into words my homeland and its history was well done and should be experienced by all whose blood runs 'Per Mare Per Terras'."

Chevalier Dr. Gregory A. McDonald, *D.D.S., K.T.J.,*
formerly *Ohio Deputy Commissioner, Clan Donald*

"An interesting personal journey, both physical and emotional, through key moments in Scottish history in '*this impersonal age/ Of mouse- clicking*' (the opposite to Burns's mouse(?), in 'Blairgowrie Hospitality'). Overmire's poetic voice is direct and at times bracingly confrontational: '*And in the end, what have we got?/ A ruin of stone/ That strangers might visit*' ('Threave Castle').

The American poet, seeking some sort of 'home' in Scotland's past, pulls together facts and dates, emotions and recollections, always with an ear/eye on literary or musical echoes. The poem 'Portree Awakening' effectively evokes The Beatles through observing children crossing the road on the Scottish island – this poet is interested in connections, not separations.

For all the bloody history and anguish reflected in the places and people Overmire encounters, there is ultimately a humanist positivity about the whole collection: '*It's true!/ Sunshine on Leith!!/ The Proclaimers knew what they were/ Talking about!*' ('Proclaim it from the Mountaintops')."

Dr. Keith Hughes, *English Literature, University of Edinburgh*

"Through haunting images painted with words... [Overmire] uncovers the heart of each place he visits and helps us know the very soul of this country. In reading his verse, we come to discern not only who the ancient Scots were, but also, who we, the descents of these often fierce people, really are. You will want to sit by the fire with a cup of hot chocolate or a wee dram, and Rabbie Burns looking over your shoulder as you revisit the places and stories of Scotland over and over in these verses."

Anita Scott-Philbrick, *Ph.D, Deputy Chieftain, Clan Scott Society*
excerpt from review, *Stag & Thistle, 2016*

THE GHOST
OF RABBIE BURNS

An American Poet's
Journey Through Scotland

Laurence Overmire

 INDELIBLE MARK PUBLISHING

Indelible Mark Publishing 2016

Editing, cover/interior design, author photo: Nancy McDonald

Front cover photo:
Burns monument at sunset in Aberdeen by Elnur/Shutterstock

Back cover photo:
The Piper at Glencoe by Laurence Overmire

All interior photos by Laurence Overmire and
Nancy McDonald unless otherwise noted

Library of Congress Control Number 2016935002

ISBN 978-0-9795398-6-2

INDELIBLE MARK PUBLISHING, LLC
West Linn, OR 97068
www.indeliblemarkpublishing.com

To my grandparents
Irl and Anna Mary (Shriver) Fast
whose Celtic roots run deep

The heart ay's the part ay,
That makes us right or wrang.
~ Robert Burns

Books of poetry by Laurence Overmire

Honor & Remembrance
A Poetic Journey through American History

Report From X-Star 10
Sci-Fi Poetry

Gone Hollywood

Videopoems by Laurence Overmire on YouTube

Ode to an Endangered Species

Maybe the Trees

Viewpoint

Beach Walk at Sunset

More books by Laurence Overmire

The One Idea That Saves the World
A Call to Conscience and A Call to Action

One Immigrant's Legacy
The Overmyer Family in America, 1751-2009

A Revolutionary American Family
The McDonalds of Somerset County, New Jersey

William R. McDonald and Abigail Fowler of
Herkimer County, New York and Their Descendants

The McDonalds of Lansingburgh, Rensselaer County,
New York
The Pioneering Family of Richard and Catharine (Lansing)
McDonald and Their Descendants

TABLE OF CONTENTS

INTRODUCTION i

PREFACE 1

The Ghost of Rabbie Burns* 9

Johnson and Boswell 11

The Unicorn Chained 13

The Bards of Scotland, Ireland and Wales* 14

The Train to Edinburgh* 16

Kenneth McKellar and I 17

Walking Through St. Giles* 19

Greyfriars Kirk and Bobby* 22

Lady Stair's Close 24

Proclaim It From The Mountaintops* 26

Don't Mess with Mons Meg 27

St. Margaret's Chapel* 28

Black Bull's Dinner* 30

Where Wizards are Born* 32

The Stone of Scone 34

Stirling Bridge* 36

The Battle of Falkirk* 37

De Bohun and De Brus* 40

The Last to Die* 43

The Royal Palace 47

Argyll's Lodging* 50

The Twa Queens of Buchlyvie* 53

* See Liner Notes for more background on these poems

Blairgowrie Hospitality*   55

Aberdeen City and Shire*   58

Never Enough Time*   60

The Clan Chief*   62

Culloden Moor*   66

When Flora Opened the Door*   68

Inverness   69

The Death of Kings*   71

The Painted People*   72

The Druid's Spell*   74

Orkney: The Wake of the Dragon's Head   75

The Loch Ness Monster   77

Epiphany on the A87   79

Eilean Donan   80

The Highland Clearances   82

Getting Away From It All   83

Portree Awakening   85

Duntulm Castle   87

Museum of Island Life*   89

Skye Lost   92

The Ornsay Lighthouse   94

Mid-Chew*   96

Armadale Castle*   98

The Museum of the Isles   100

Ferry To Lochaber   102

The Light of Iona   106

* See Liner Notes for more background on these poems

Oban 109

Inviting Inveraray 111

Harry Potter's Jacobite Steam Train 113

Caledonian Mad Car Disease* 114

The Piper at Glencoe* 116

Luss on Loch Lomond* 119

The Governor of Dumbarton* 122

Glasgow Sunrise 124

An Ayrshire Farm 127

St. Bride's Kirk* 129

One Morning in Laurieston* 135

Coffee in Kirkcudbright 140

Threave Castle* 143

Down in Dumfries* 147

Murder in the Church* 149

Lady Devorgilla's Bridge* 152

Burns House 154

Universal Brotherhood* 157

The Yes and No Campaign* 159

The Burns Who Crossed the Ocean* 162

PHOTO ALBUM 163

LINER NOTES 173

ABOUT THE AUTHOR 191

* See Liner Notes for more background on these poems

INTRODUCTION

HOW I DID *NOT* MANAGE TO MEET LAURENCE OVERMIRE

...when, with his wife Nancy McDonald, he visited Galloway where I live, is a story he tells in the liner notes to his new collection of poetry. He is a true *sennachie*, a genealogist as well as a bard. This publication documents his first-ever visit to Old Caledonia. Subtitled *An American Poet's Journey Through Scotland*, his book permits us to travel in his genial, self-effacing company during the lead-up to the independence referendum of 2014 and to see something of our country through his American eyes. We can all recognize his picture of sungleam on the Forth when viewed from Edinburgh Castle in his "Proclaim it From the Mountains." We meet Harry Potter squeezed in between the Douglas Black Dinner and the Stone of Destiny. He is back with "The Battle of Falkirk" proclaiming that *"Freedom is an idea/That no tyrant will ever crush,"* a welcome recurrent theme throughout.

A visit to Flodden Field inspires a plea for the eradication of war. "Never Enough Time" beautifully captures the frustration of the tourist who has to miss out on some sites. *"The real glare of gone yesterday"* (p. 71) strikes me as truly insightful. Knocked out by Orkney, as who would not be, he and Nancy rejoice that *"Nothing is of the ordinary"* (p. 76).

It is truly refreshing to encounter an American celebrating the absence of billboards and adverts when driving through the country: *"Guess what, Toto?!/We're not in America anymore!"* "The Highland Clearances" sounds a sympathetic chord but avoids the sad truth that hardly any of the exiles have ever displayed much of a desire to return. Like many of us he finds Skye entrancing, if somewhat baffling in contemplating "*human inadequacy on the/Precipitous edge of/Survival,*" which neatly chimes with "*What myths do we tell ourselves/Now/That prevent us from finding/The truth?*"

"Caledonian Mad Car Disease" is hilarious, well-crafted and attractively self-deflationary. Moving to the southwest he captures the power of Threave Castle and the depression that many detect in Dumfries, though somewhat tempered by the spirit of Burns:

> *How many countries*
> *Would you guess*
> *Have a poet*
> *As their national hero?*

Laurence and Nancy went looking for her ancestry in Laurieston or Clachanpluck as it was known before it received its gentrified renaming. Galloway's best known writer, S. R. Crockett, was a lousy poet but an accomplished novelist. Many of his stories are set in his native Glenkens and he often gave many places known to him "ghost names." One of them was Pluckemin, which is mentioned twice in his novel *The Standard Bearer* (1898). At p. 202 he mentions "*the clachan of Pluckemin*" and at p. 248, "*the Four Roads of Pluckemin.*" The place actually did exist – it was a ferm-toun on the Bargatton property but it never possessed four roads, while nearby Laurieston, or Clachanpluck two miles away, did. The main revelation of Laurence's "One Morning in Laurieston" is that there is a place in New Jersey named Pluckemin. Crockett reported a tradition that the Griersons of Bargatton emigrated to America in 1708, so Nancy definitely did come home.

This is a memorable and skillful collection which admirably manages to capture some of the idiosyncrasies of both Scotland and America. It is to be hoped that it will find an appreciative readership on both sides of the Atlantic.

Ted Cowan
Emeritus professor of Scottish history and literature
University of Glasgow

PREFACE

This is a journal of a sojourn to Scotland, a return to the home of my ancestors.

Like Johnson and Boswell, those intrepid chroniclers of Scotland in 1773,[1] I was on a journey of discovery. I didn't know what I would find on this my very first visit to my ancestral home, but something told me I would find a long lost part of myself.

You see, my ancestors may have left Scotland hundreds of years ago, but Scotland hasn't left me. I am tied somehow. And I knew I must return, having been cast out for so long from the motherland that, in some mysterious way, made me what I am today.

The clans are in my blood: Burns, Buchanan, Scott, Douglas, Colquhoun, Pollock, McKibben, Matthews, Baird, Thomson, Edmonstone, and many much more ancient: MacDonald, Hamilton, Campbell, Sinclair, Keith, Fraser, Erskine, Boyd, Graham, Wallace and Stewart. And that's but a wee dram of who I am.

I know these things because I am a genealogist. I have traced my ancestry far far back in time – to Robert the Bruce, John "The Red" Comyn, James "The Black" Douglas, William the Lion, Somerled, Malcolm III and Kenneth McAlpin.[2] They are all somehow a part of me, and they all had a part to play in my return to my ancient roots.

---

[1] In 1773, the writers, James Boswell, a Scotsman, and Samuel Johnson, an Englishman, toured Scotland from Edinburgh to Aberdeen, Inverness and various islands of the Hebrides including Skye and Mull. In 1785, Boswell published *The Journal of a Tour to the Hebrides with Samuel Johnson, LL.D.*

[2] In America, thanks to effective record keeping, lineages can often be reliably traced back to the earliest immigrants in the 1600's, many of whom came from aristocratic backgrounds. It is not unusual for

My great grandmother was Mary Isabelle Burns Shriver. Her family tradition claimed our Burns family was related to the poet Robert Burns. Indeed, as early as 1888, an article appeared in the monthly periodical *Reformed Presbyterian and Covenanter* reporting that "Rev. John Cuthbertson came from Scotland as the first Covenanter missionary in America. He brought with him a small colony of people, the most distinguished member of which was his brother-in-law, Archibald Bourns, the progenitor of the Burns family..."[3] They settled in the vicinity of Gettysburg, Pennsylvania, the same general area from whence my Burns ancestors came.

In 1910, Charles W. Cremer, editor of the *Waynesboro Record,* delivered an address to the Kittochtinny Historical Society stating that two uncles of Robert Burns came to America – Thomas Bourns in 1747 and Archibald Bourns (mentioned above) in 1751.[4] Cremer claimed to have established the relationships from records in London and Edinburgh:

"The inquiry led to records in London and in Edinburgh and, after long waiting, established the fact that Archibald Bourns was a brother of William Burness, the father of Robert Burns."[5]

Americans to discover that they are descended from King Edward I or Edward III of England and Robert the Bruce of Scotland with ancestral lines going all the way back to Charlemagne, from whom virtually the entire European monarchy is descended.

[3] Rev. W. M. Glasgow, "Covenanters at Gettysburg," *Reformed Presbyterian and Covenanter,* Vol. XXVI, No. 10, Oct 1888.

[4] Charles W. Cremer, "A Franklin County Cousin of Robert Burns," an address to the Kittochtinny Historical Society, *Waynesboro Record,* Waynesboro, Franklin Co., PA, Feb 2, 1910.

[5] Ibid. Unfortunately, Mr. Cremer did not provide any documentation to support his claims.

Archibald Bourns' wife was Janet Cuthbertson, a sister of Rev. John Cuthbertson. A well-researched and documented book by S. Helen Fields published in 1934 reaffirmed the story of the two uncles adding some more detail about the Cuthbertsons.

According to Ms. Fields, Rev. Dr. John Cuthbertson was born near Ayr, Ayrshire, Scotland, on Apr. 3, 1718.[6] (The poet Robert Burns was born in Alloway, Ayrshire, on Jan. 25, 1759.) Cuthbertson's job was to minister to Scottish Covenanters in Pennsylvania who had been persecuted in the Old Country. On his voyage to America in 1751, he was accompanied by his sister, Janet Cuthbertson Bourns, and her husband, Archibald Bourns, of Lanark, Scotland, with their infant son, John. Archibald, Ms. Fields affirms was the second brother of William Burness, the father of the poet Robert Burns. The family settled on a farm on what is now part of the Gettysburg Battlefield. Thomas, the other uncle of Robert Burns, settled in Mifflin County, Pennsylvania, in 1747.[7]

As a genealogist, I have not been able to prove the validity of the Burns heritage one way or the other. Proof is very hard to come by in genealogy. Time has a way of wiping out historical truth. Documentary evidence is often very difficult to find.

My earliest known Burns ancestor is said to be John Burns (c. 1745-c. 1791) of Franklin County, Pennsylvania. He may have been related to Archibald or Thomas, but John's parents have not yet been positively identified. But whether or not Robert Burns is a fairly close blood relation

---

[6] Rev. John Cuthbertson and S. Helen Fields, *Register of Marriages and Baptisms Performed by Rev. John Cuthbertson* (Genealogical Publishing Co., Baltimore, originally published in Washington D.C., 1934), vii. Rev. Cuthbertson kept a detailed diary, which recorded his birth date.
[7] Ibid, xi-xii.

of mine, he is certainly a kindred spirit and a guiding voice within my poetic conscience, and has been for a very long time.

Traditionally, we human beings have placed an awful lot of significance on being related to people by blood. But is this emphasis misleading or misplaced?

The truth of our ancestry is that we are all related. All of us are, in fact, literally cousins.[8] That's the plain truth that we need to recognize and make conscious. As a poet, I have learned to appreciate all my relations going all the way back in time - embracing the entirety of our common humanity. We are all brothers and sisters. And every creature, even the smallest mouse as the poet tells us, has its sacred place in the scheme of things. Robert Burns, like so many other admirable people before him, reminded us of this great truth. Then, as now, too few are listening or paying attention.

Thankfully, on this journey to Scotland in September of 2014, I was accompanied by my wife, Nancy McDonald. Yes or No was the big question in Scotland at the time. Should the country become independent of Britain or not? Doors of opportunity occasionally open as we make our way in this life. Do we choose to go through the door or not?

Our questions were not primarily political, however. We were on a much more personal quest to discover the truth of Nancy's Scottish heritage, which centered around a place called Pluckamin near Laurieston in Dumfries and Galloway. The fascinating insights we gained from that quest were published in 2015 in *A Revolutionary American Family: The McDonalds of Somerset County, New Jersey*, a

---

[8] DNA reveals that we all share common ancestors in Africa about 60,000 years ago. See *Deep Ancestry: Inside the Genographic Project*, by Spencer Wells (National Geographic, 2006).

book we are proud to say is now on the shelf in the library at Clan Donald Skye. Nancy's McDonald ancestor, we believe, fled Scotland in the company of Lord Neil Campbell, the brother of the 9th Earl of Argyll, during the "Killing Time" of 1685, when fanatic religious fervor and persecution were at their worst.[9]

Times have changed. People have evolved. The Scottish people and Scottish ideas have played a large part in the world's transformation.[10] Robert Burns' call for Universal Brotherhood, along with the enlightened thinking of so many other compassionate visionaries, has had a dramatic impact on modern thinking and behavior. The Scottish values of fairness, justice, equality, hard work and education have led the way to a higher quality of human life and global prosperity.

These threads will all weave themselves throughout the poetic narrative of my journey, a journey which began here in America years before, as I first put pen to paper to explore that unrequited yearning to reconnect with my Scottish heritage, particularly in regards to my grandmother, Anna Mary Shriver Fast, the daughter of Mary Isabelle Burns Shriver. She was my most direct link to my Scottish past.

The journey continued with a plane flight to London, a train to Edinburgh and a whirlwind of adventure through much of Scotland, from Stirling and Perth to Culloden, Inverness and Skye, Loch Lomond to Glasgow, Kirkcudbright and Dumfries.

---

[9] Archibald Campbell, 9th Earl of Argyll, was beheaded for being one of the leaders of the Monmouth Rebellion to overthrow King James II.

[10] A good book on this subject is Arthur Herman's *How the Scots Invented the Modern World: The True Story of How Western Europe's Poorest Nation Created Our World and Everything in It* (Broadway Books, 2002).

It was a journey my wife Nancy and I will never forget. These are my experiences, thoughts, reflections and hopes for the future, when Universal brother- and sisterhood will truly manifest upon our Earth.

We invite you now to come along with us, tune an ear to the telling, and enjoy the ride.

Laurence Overmire
West Linn, Oregon, USA

Journal

THE GHOST OF RABBIE BURNS

My grandmother Mary
Somewhat bitterly recalled
How the family was
Swindled, by an unscrupulous
Brother-in-law who stole
The family inheritance through
A trickery of legal wrangling.

But he was just a businessman
Doing what comes naturally
Making money fist over hand

While she was a dreamer
With a poet's heart

In the fields with her sister
Painting cornstalks
Singing songs in the parlor
The moon peeping through the window...

Not for her, the dreary
Ashland farm, rain-soaked in
Ohio.

No.

She belonged to another world:
A mansion high on a Scottish hill
With a great wooden staircase and
Curling banister

Where, in a rocker by the fire, on cold
Winter evenings, the ghost of
Rabbie Burns would set her
On his knee and whisper

Stories of the Highlands.

She married a teacher
A man of honor and little money
And lived a simple life
Nothing fancy, no, but sure
There can be no doubt that
In the end

Hers was a dream worth keeping.

Johnson and Boswell
Touring the Hebrides

In 1773

Dr. Samuel Johnson, celebrated author and
James Boswell, lawyer and diarist
Toured the Highlands and the Hebrides
Met Flora and Allan MacDonald in Kingsburgh

On Skye

A difficult time for them, as it was
The MacDonalds' fortunes sinking
After farming failures at Flodigarry

One year later
Flora and Allan moved
To North Carolina
In America
Just in time to catch
The Revolution
And the desperate
Heartbreak of war

Johnson and Boswell
Left a record of a time and place
For the future to digest

I leave a record, too

My journey from the Lowlands
To the Highlands
A fishhook through the
Heart of the land
Learning along the way
Taking note of the expression
Of a culture
The feeling of a people
The aspirations of a time

Years hence
Some will appreciate
Some will disregard
Some won't even take
Notice

But for those who care
Something will be shared
Something these words
Will never be able to

Encompass or explain.

THE UNICORN CHAINED

A free Unicorn
Is a dangerous creature
According to legend

That's why you'll find
In the halls of the Scottish kings
The mythical beast is
Collared 'round the throat
A bright gold chain
Attached

Woven into tapestries
Molded into statuary

A symbol of great healing power
Of innocence, joy, purity
Intelligence and
Sovereign might

A magical animal
Rearing on its haunches
That only the realm of
The Gaels
Could tame

Fantasy
Myth
Legend
Truth

All are intertwined in the story
That is Scotland.

THE BARDS OF SCOTLAND, IRELAND AND WALES

The Bard, like the Piper, was
A high status individual
Within a Celtic Clan

The Bards were the poets
The keepers of history
And oral tradition
Maintaining the memory of the
Sacredness of the Word

They knew the lineage
Of the families
The births and the deaths
The stories
That linked the generations

They stood by the Chief
And followed him into battle
Bearing witness to the scene
Observing and taking note
The experience to be later
Remembered and honored
In poetry and song

They were the intellectual
Leaders
The conscience of the
World
Highly respected
Regarded with reverence

When the Bard gave voice
From the fire in his heart
The people were compelled
To listen

Alas, these purveyors of
Truth have long since
Disappeared

Their absence today
Is a warning
To us all:

A society that has no respect
No regard
For its Bards
Its historians, its storytellers
Is a society in steep decline
A society that has lost its
Very soul

And may never find its way.

THE TRAIN TO EDINBURGH

Leaving London
Watching the countryside
Change

From Peterborough
To Doncaster
To Wakefield
Leeds
York
Darlington
Newcastle

And finally passing into
Scotland
For the very first time

This is the return
After so many hundreds of
Years

All of my ancestors are with me
Burns, Scott, Douglass,
Colquhoun, Buchanan, Baird,
Pollock, McKibben and Thomson

As the door opens
My foot steps down on
Solid ground

Home.

KENNETH McKELLAR AND I

Walked the Royal Mile
Together

There he was singing inside my head:

"Oh, let me walk the Royal Mile that's Scotland's brave
highway,
Where at one o'clock from the Castle Rock comes auld
Reekie's call each day;
And as the echo sounds in the Palace grounds then the
heavens on Scotland smile;
And you'll make your day in the royal way on the Royal
Mile."

He and I
Go way way back
You see
Whenever I yearned to re-connect
With my bonnie homeland

I turned on his golden voice
Taking me away
"Like a bird on the wing"

In the old days it was a cassette
(The young ones don't even know
What that is)

Later it was a CD
Until that too
Became irrelevant

Now I have him on a digital cloud

"O, my love is like a red, red rose
That's newly sprung in June"

He's no longer with us
In flesh
May he rest in peace

But his voice still rings
Anytime you need him
He'll always be there

And that's why I say
Though I never once met him
He is nonetheless

My very good friend.

WALKING THROUGH ST. GILES

Is to be engulfed in the
Enormity of Scottish
History

Moving from the light of day
Into the interior darkness
Of the magnificent Kirk

Like entering a holy
Womb where new ideas
Were given birth

Above us is the
Stained glass window
Devoted to the poetry of

Robert Burns

Depicting his
Green natural world
Celebrating the unity of all
Humankind
One family, together
Regardless of race or color
Or creed

A life of love
Like a red, red rose

A statue in the corner
Of dark, glaring wood

Its finger pointing to the holy
Book
This is John Knox
Fiery Presbyterian
Preacher

Outside he's buried in the
Car park

The Reformation brought
New divisions
Spiritually and culturally
A National Covenant in 1638

Everyone asking questions
Searching for the answers
That would lead them
To God

Scathing, vituperous politics erupted into
War

The 1st Marquess of Argyll
Archibald Campbell
Led the Covenanting Reformers

He rests in effigy along the wall

His rival, the Great Montrose
The Royalist leader
Rests much in the same way
On the opposite wall

Two men beheaded for their
Opposite convictions

Times have changed
Thank God

The church now brings them all
Together
Those who might think and believe
Different things
In the Robert Burns' way of
Universal brother- and sisterhood

St. Giles continues to be a
Spiritual home
Giving hope for a world we can all
Believe in

Despite the conflict of its past
When you walk inside
You will find love and
Peace there

Today.

GREYFRIARS KIRK AND BOBBY

One of the oldest surviving buildings
In Edinburgh
Dating back to 1620

The National Covenant was signed here
In front of the pulpit
In 1638

A societal revolution was underway
A revolution of thinking and ideas

Painful though it would prove
Convulsing three kingdoms in
Bloody civil wars
Eventually the ideas of equality
And social justice
Would move the whole world

Forward

Today, the Kirk is beautiful and
Welcoming inside
Their message is one of peace
And tranquility

Outside, a walk in the graveyard
Is a humbling experience
We all have so little time on this
Earth
Precious little time

Covenanters were once held in a prison
In the corner of the churchyard
They say it is a haunted place
Surely injustice toward any of our
Fellow human beings
Should haunt us all
Now and forevermore

Greyfriar's Bobby
The famous Skye Terrier
Is remembered here
For 14 years he kept vigil
By his master's gravestone

Love is a powerful thing
It transcends time and place
If you're looking for immortality
Love long and love well

The rest will take care of itself.

LADY STAIR'S CLOSE
Edinburgh

Three great Scottish writers
Robert Burns
Sir Walter Scott
Robert Louis Stevenson

Celebrated in
The Writer's Museum
In Lady Stair's House
Built in 1622

Portraits, busts
Objects and
Writings

The lives of three great men
Are partially revealed in
Fragments
Of their time on this
Earth

What will be left of us
You and I?
If anything
Hundreds of years
From now

"We are such stuff
As dreams are made on"

Another great writer said.

The books may find themselves
Neglected and forgotten
On dusty shelves
But there will always be thinkers
Dreamers
Lovers

They will find a way to truth

They will give the spark
To another age
And another celebration
Of what it means
To be alive.

Proclaim It From The Mountaintops

Atop Edinburgh Castle
On the parapet from which
Mons Meg looms
With a threatening pow'r
Looking north
On a cloudy day

Suddenly the sun comes out
But the beams streaming in
Are blocked by the enormity
Of the castle rock
Casting a vast shadow on the
City below

Darkness everywhere
Except
There
On the Firth of Forth
There is a band of sunshine
On the river edge
The light breaking across
From the top of the
Mount

You don't believe me?

It's true!

Sunshine on Leith!!

The Proclaimers knew what they were
Talking about!

DON'T MESS WITH MONS MEG

Gifted to James II
By Philip the Good, Duke of Burgundy
In 1454

15,000 pounds of iron
15 feet long

A 400 pound cannon ball
Does wonders for a castle's
Complexion

Now the king could rightly say
He had the biggest damn balls
In Scotland!

ST. MARGARET'S CHAPEL
Edinburgh Castle

The oldest building in Scotland now
A holy place
Named for a holy sister
Princess
Of the House of Wessex

Ferry me there
'Cross the Firth of Forth
The pilgrim's path from
Dunfermline
To pay respects

To those who shine the light
In the darkest times
The darkest ages of Man
When there is little hope
Of salvation

Rest in this quiet place
A simple
Yet elegant
Refuge
From the storm

A thousand years of tears
Have dried upon its floor
A humble offering
Well fit for a Queen and her
King

Margaret died shortly after hearing
Of her husband Malcolm's death
In battle, in Alnwick, in 1093
The devout heart
Finally

Broken.

Give her a prayer
Before you leave
Give her a blessing
A small gift of thanks
To remember her by.

BLACK BULL'S DINNER

How do you get rid of a
Rival?

Invite him to dinner

That's what the wily Chancellor
Sir William Crichton did
Acting in the interests, he might say
Of the 10-year-old King James II
(Great great grandfather of Mary
Queen of Scots)

16-year-old William Douglas
Was a wealthy young noble
Too rich and too powerful
And a great grandson of Robert III
To boot

Time to stop these Douglases
While we still can, Crichton must have
Thought
And why not invite his brother
14-year-old David, too

The unsuspecting boys were fed
Right royally
Until the final course was laid
Before them
A black bull's head
Signifying someone's imminent
Death

Seized, accused of treason
Dragged into the courtyard and
Beheaded
The threatening reach of the Black Douglases
Was severed

Such was the power of kings.

And what perchance
Was in store for the rest of us

For dessert?

WHERE WIZARDS ARE BORN

It's interesting to think
How some things come to
Pass

Imagine
In a restaurant
A woman writing with a notepad

Day after day, hour upon hour
She comes
Dutifully
An unknown passion driving her

Who is she?
What is her story?

A nobody?
Like the rest of us?

Later, the world discovers
What it was that was in her head
And needed so furiously
To get out –

Harry Potter.

Now everyone goes to the
Restaurant
Wanting to somehow touch

That story

And become a wizard
Themselves.

THE STONE OF SCONE

The Stone of Destiny

The embodiment and symbol
Of Scotland and its ancient

History and culture

When Edward I
The Hammer of the Scots
Took the Stone of Scone
Away from its people
In 1296
He put it underneath
The Coronation Chair
Of England

The metaphor should not
Escape us

It was an act of conquest
And defiance

Time will pass
Meanings will shift

Now we must come to terms
All of us

With what subjugation and
Equality
In a healthy democratic
State

Really mean.

STIRLING BRIDGE
11 Sept. 1297

William Wallace was a giant
Of a man, they say
Well over six feet tall

He and Sir Andrew Moray
Were determined to
Stop the English
Where the Bridge
Crossed the River Forth

They refused the entreaty
To surrender

"Tell your commander
That we are not here to make peace
But to do battle, defend ourselves and
Liberate our kingdom.
Let them come on, and we shall prove
This in their very beards."

The English knights
Crossed

The Scottish attacked
And cut them off at the
Neck of the bridge
A stranglehold that
Proved the English
Undoing

The fight for freedom was on...

THE BATTLE OF FALKIRK
22 July 1298

Ten months after Stirling Bridge –

Disaster.

Wallace's army
Mostly peasants
Was vastly outnumbered
Jealous nobles envious of his success
Refusing to support him

Only the Red Comyn joined him
Holding his cavalry in reserve

The Hammer of the Scots
Edward I was determined
To crush this brave heart
Utterly

He brought with him
2,500 heavily armored knights
12,500 infantry
English, Welsh and Irish
A host of archers armed with
Longbows
And the loyal contingents of eight
Noble Earls

Wallace had planned well
Skillfully employing
The circular formation
Known as the schiltron

His men armed with 12 foot
Spears formed tight
Impenetrable units and
Held their ground

Those spears like porcupines
Impaling horse and rider
As the English charged
Without effect

But the noble Comyn and his men
Instead of engaging at this
Critical venture
Withdrew and rode away

Leaving Wallace and his
Peasant army
To their own unpropitious
Fate

A hail of iron-tipped arrows
From the English longbows
Cut through the thicket of schiltrons
And left the Scots exposed

One more charge
From the heavily armored
Knights sent the survivors
Fleeing for the lives

Wallace escaped
But not for long

His power was broken
At least in that place and time

He was executed as a traitor
In August 1307
Drawn and quartered in the most
Horrific of deaths

But nothing it seems
Could stop the beating of that
Fierce
Unwavering
Heart

Freedom is an idea
That no tyrant will ever crush.

DE BOHUN AND DE BRUS
At Bannockburn
23 June 1314

Nobleman to nobleman
Might the battle be waged
Brief though the window of
Opportunity be

There the king sits
Astride a palfrey
And there might he die
No match for an armored
Knight on an English
Warhorse
Bred to the bone of
Chivalry

Spur to the hide
Lance leveled
Young blood's impetuous
Charge
On to death and glory

The gallant De Bohun to
Make history

The Bruce
Seeing the ghost
Ride out of the mist
Thundering hooves pounding
Turned
Breast open to the challenger

Calmly waiting to meet
His foe
The lance bearing down
With deadly intent

As the last second paused
A quick twist in the saddle
Horse nimbly wheeled
And a great arm lifted
Axe in hand
One sweeping blow
And down went De Bohun
Skull cleaved in two

The English hope
Lay dead on the field
The battle was already decided
Cunning and courage would win
The day
And arrogance, mighty in show
But weak in heart and head
Would beat
Its fast retreat

A schiltron's nest of poor
Unheralded farmers, craftsmen
Builders and believers
The true blood of Scotland
Sent their message

To all who would be crowned in
Oppression, injustice
And greed
You will not take this land
You will not break this people
Not now
Not ever
While yet we stand
United and

Defiant.

THE LAST TO DIE
Flodden Field, 1513

The memorial stands
On a remote, forsaken hill
Near Branxton
Northumberland
England

9 September 1513

King James IV of Scotland
Met the Earl of Surrey
On this long forgotten field
The largest battle ever fought
Between these two
Kingdoms

Henry VIII
Busy in France
Fighting to make a name for
Himself
Claimed himself Overlord
Of the Scottish realm
A bold affront to the
Scottish king

The politics of the day
Are obscure and obtuse
Treaties and alliances
The War of the League of Cambrai
Emperor Maximilian
The siege of Thérouanne

Pope Leo X, King Louis XII
Henry and James

A colossal collision of
Uncompromising
Egos

James invaded England

The battle of Flodden
Ended in a gallant charge
Led by regal James
Straight into the teeth
Of the waiting Surrey

An arrow and a bill
Brought the King to the
Ground
Gallant to the last
His valiant fight worthy of a
Bardic ode

But what was the cost?

10,000 Scots they say
Gave their lives that day
The cream of the Scottish
Nobility

How many wives were left widows?
How many children fatherless?

For what?

*"The Floo'ers o' the Forest
Are a' wede away"*

The costs of war are
Impossible to
Measure
Generations hence
Must pay the
Price

James IV was the last
Monarch
To die
In battle
In Britain

Leaders in modern times
Never expose themselves
To death
How easy can it be to push
A button
And watch others die
In your place?

Let Flodden be a warning
To all those
Who would make war
Unnecessarily

We have had enough of such
Wars
Wars as political feud
Overblown ambition
And nonsensical
Game playing
Powerful chessmen
Lining their own pockets

The real heroes
Wield no weapons
Other than a sharpened mind
And a grateful heart
They toil endlessly
To prevent
Wars from ever happening
Bridging differences through
Peaceful means

Do not disrespect those
Who fell at Flodden
They died with courage, no doubt
Honor and
Remember their sacrifice
And learn the lessons
They gave their lives
To teach.

THE ROYAL PALACE
Stirling Castle

Stunning!

A Renaissance gem

Newly restored to its former
Grandeur
In all of its magnificent
Splendor

The palace looks now
As it might have looked
In 1545

The home of King James V and his wife
Mary of Guise
The parents of Mary, Queen of Scots

Wealthy, learned, sophisticated

These were not crude, barbarian
Rubes
Living in the dark, drab medieval
Spaces of cold, uncultured Europe

Bright colors, ornate tapestries
Rich fabrics
Artful decorations

A ceiling of carved heads
Beautifully painted
Kings and queens of Scotland

Emperors of ancient Rome
Heroes of the Bible

James V became King at
17 months old
After his father, James IV
Was killed at Flodden Field
His mother, Margaret, was the sister
Of Henry VIII

James's palace was his crowning
Glory

A lover and patron of
Poetry and music
He died of an illness
At the age of 30

His daughter, Mary
Becoming
Queen
At 6 days old

They come to life here
Ghosts walking
In the re-enacted flair of
Ages past

Be wary where you step
The Swiss Guard is on
Alert and waiting...

The Palace at Stirling

Of all the extraordinary
Castles in Scotland

This timeless treasure
Must be savored
To be believed.

ARGYLL'S LODGING

Archibald Campbell
The 9th Earl of Argyll

Lived with his wife
Anna McKenzie
At Argyll's Lodging
Near Stirling Castle

The most important surviving
Townhouse of its period
In Scotland

Anna ran the household
While her husband was oft away
On business

The house has the feel of
Comfortable, but tasteful
Luxury
So well put together
Confident, but not obnoxious

The 9th Earl was the son of
Archibald, 1st Marquess of Argyll
The most powerful man in Scotland
In his day
Leader of the Covenanter movement
Who was beheaded in 1661
By King Charles II of England
For collaborating with Cromwell's
Cold and calculating
Commonwealth

Complicated politics, truly

This was an age of religious and
Regal
Fanaticism

The 9th Earl got caught in the
Middle
Trying to find moderation in a world gone
Nuts

Unable to dance his way 'round
The political obstacle course
He stumbled and stepped on
Too many toes
And was beheaded himself for treason
In 1685
For backing the Monmouth Rebellion
To contest the throne of
King James II

Fanatic thinking gives rise to
Tyrants
Cruelty
Barbarism
Injustice

All, unbelievably, in the name of God

The feverish pitch of the
17th century
Sent many to America
To try something new

Argyll's Lodging, however
Was an oasis of clarity
In a sea of darkness

The women, perhaps
Like Anna McKenzie Campbell
Understood much better than
The men
That
Only through tolerance
Kindness
Understanding and forgiveness
Can we build a house
Of love and
Find our way to

Sanity.

THE TWA QUEENS OF BUCHLYVIE

Tired and footsore
From a day of sightseeing
At Stirling
We stepped into a small bistro
In the out of the way town
Of Buchlyvie
For a late afternoon
Spot of tea

Two elderly ladies
Sat nearby
Rather royally
Dressed
In their church-going best

Partaking of the sunny
Sunday sunshine
Pouring through
The seemingly seamless window
Overlooking the garden
And the freshly mown fields
Of hay

One was a local
And one lived in Canada

When we told them
We were from Oregon
The Canadian lady
Said she had a relative
In Oregon in Lake Oswego

Well, wouldn't you know
Lake Oswego is just down
The road from our lovely
Abode

How nice
How quaint
How fun!

The Twa Queens
Laughed
Unabashedly

And so did we!

BLAIRGOWRIE HOSPITALITY

In this impersonal age
Of mouse-clicking
Finger-linking of
Intertwining
Virtual relationship

Occasionally

In the spanning of
Intercontinental
Divides

You meet

Someone off the grid and
In the flesh

And so it was
We being in need
Of a place to stay
My sister introduced us
(In a wave of cyberspace)
To her Scottish Facebook friend
Dianne of Blairgowrie

She and her son
Took us in
(as old friends might)
To her lovely
Springbank Cottage
Nestled off to the side
Of a country road

Just down the way
From Perth

Weary travelers we were
After battling the traffic in
Edinburgh
Beating the heat
At Bannockburn
And scaling the heights of
Stirling Castle

The room was all ready for us
Neatly prepared
A beautiful upstairs nook
With a window overlooking
The garden

There was even a basket of
Carefully selected necessaries
Waiting on the nightstand to
Welcome us
To our temporary
Home

Our hosts knew a great place
For dinner, too
A local favorite
Just a short stroll away
On a mystical moonlit night
The breeze just enough to
Glance the skin and pique
The sense of divinity

The chef was ready and able
To cater
To our every
Plant-based need
(Aware of our concerns
For health, for animals and for
The well being of a planet
Imperiled by climate change)

He served a special creation
Just for us

We wined
We dined
We became great friends

That's the wonder of
Scottish hospitality
That made our visit
To this enchanted land
Truly remarkable and
Everlastingly

Memorable.

ABERDEEN CITY AND SHIRE

Aberdeen
The Silver City with the Golden Sands
Between the Rivers Dee and Don
The third most populous city in
Scotland

Home to
The University of Aberdeen
Founded 1495
Scotland's third oldest
After St. Andrews and Glasgow

Engage your mind at the
Satrosphere
(Yes, you heard that right
Sat-ro-sphere)
Science and Discovery Centre
With exhibitions, workshops and
Experiments for all ages

Then there's the Aberdeen Art Gallery
The Maritime Museum
The David Welch Winter Gardens
The Gordon Highlanders Museum
Or the fascinating
Provost Skene's House

In the greater shire are some of the most
Gorgeous and majestic castles you'll find
Anywhere
The Royal residence of Balmoral
Drum Castle

Castle Fraser
And Crathes Castle
Haunted by
The Green Lady

South of Stonehaven
You'll find
Dunnottar Castle
Formidably situated
On the top of a cliff
Surrounded on three sides by
The North Sea
The stronghold of the
Keiths, the Earls Marischal
The place where the
Scottish Crown Jewels
Were hidden and kept safe
From Oliver Cromwell's
Invading army
In the 17th century

With so much to see and
So much to do
Your most difficult decision
Is trying to figure out

Exactly where to start.

NEVER ENOUGH TIME

Wheeling through the countryside
From Buchlyvie to Perth to
Blairgowrie and Pitlochrie

There's never enough time
To do what we'd like to do
To stop for a visit of more
Than an hour or two

Each place with its own culture
Its own "feel"
Its own charm

But there is no time!

We passed by Scone Palace
No time for St. Andrews
For Glamis or Blair

There's never enough time!

Somehow
We must make time

This little life
Too quick it passes

Despite the pressing insistence
Of the ordinary and the
Mundane

We must make the best time
Of the time we have
Before the tick tick ticking
Ends.

THE CLAN CHIEF

Looking smart in his tricorn hat
And trousers
Pulled me out of a group of tourists
At Culloden and
Said
"You sir! You look like my tacksman."

And so I did.
Not knowing quite
What this was all about
I was hoping to just sit and watch
An entertaining demonstration.

But it was not to be.

I was front and center.
I was a tacksman!
I'm not sure what that was
But the Clan Chief
Told me I was a wealthy
Man
I collected the rents
From all the sub-tenants
Who I could keep securely under
My thumb.

It felt pretty good to be a
Tacksman, I must say.
The clan system was not so
Bad
For a fellow like me.

And then the Clan Chief
Said he needed another
"Volunteer"
As he called him.
A peasant who I could order around.
A poor, sorry sort
Who was obligated to put
His life on the line
Whenever the Clan Chief
Had need of his services.

A young lad
With a camera
Stepped out of the crowd
And sheepishly took his
Place
Beside me.

Then the Clan Chief
Laid out the situation before us.
We were going to war
To fight for Bonnie Prince Charlie
At Culloden.

He handed me a musket.
He gave my peasant a basket hilt
Sword and a shield.

The government redcoats
Were stretched out before us.

The Clan Chief ordered me
To advance.

I stepped forward
Raised my musket
Took aim at the
Duke of Cumberland.
The Clan Chief
Said
"If you pick him off
We can all go home."

I missed.

Granted the Duke was on
Horseback trapped inside
A painting
But the imagination being
What it is
I had become one with the illusion
And was not about to be
Cheated
Of my fantasy.

We gave our best Highland yell
And pounded our shields
But the redcoats in the painting
Weren't about to budge
So
The Clan Chief charged
With one mighty flourish of his flashing
Sword

The peasant following close
Behind him
Down the carpet
And straight for the wall!

(With me holding fast
To the rear
To await the outcome)

Alas, the Clan Chief fell.

"That's it, boys, the battle
Is over for you,"
He said, rising from the dead.
"You have to wait until some
Other chieftain takes command
And tells you what to do."

The Clan Chief
With a discourteous wave of his arm
Destroyed the illusion
Dismissed me and my peasant
Banished us to the ranks of the
Here and now
And we became befuddled
Tourists once again.

So ended my foray into the
Breach at Culloden.
I was one of the lucky ones.
I didn't get killed.

CULLODEN MOOR
16 Apr 1746

Face to the wind in bitter cold
Beards crusted with ice
Gray eyes steeled in fierce rebellion
No foreign blade to master
The proud beating of a stout Highland heart.

The kilted clans had banned together
MacDonald and Fraser, Cameron and Stewart
A Bonnie Prince to lead them
Outnumbered, yet undaunted
Flags defiantly unfurled
A shaft of courage to drive sweet freedom
Home.

The bagpipe sounds its thrilling tune
The ranks in line of tartan shield
English cannon pounding
From generation to generation
Father and son
Kinsman and brother
A slow steady advance and

Charge!

Across the sodden moor
Broadswords waving
Over the blood-stained ground
A gallant fight of hand-to-hand
And death
At last succumbing
An hundred years and more...

No more.

The final thrust of grim Fate's story
Here
Upon a Scots grave field of
Honor.

WHEN FLORA OPENED THE DOOR

At the Bonnie Prince there standing
The blood of war hard upon his face
His eyes defeated, all hope lost

She covered his pain in a blanket
As best she could
Water to drink and a bit of bread

Ferried him across in the dark of night
The breaking heart of Skye
Set him down on a farther shore

The sun of some other day to come, surely
She thought, as winter before spring
When the bloom of the heather will

Take the hill and dance with the bagpipe
Again.

INVERNESS

The capital of the Highlands
At the mouth of the River Ness
In olden times 'twas a
Stronghold of the Picts

St. Columba himself journeyed here
To convert the Pictish King Brude

Denied entry by the king
Columba knocked and the doors
Mysteriously open'd!

Macbeth, Shakespeare's tragic
Scottish brute
As Mormaer of Moray and Ross
At a later date
Held a castle within the city

Then Malcolm III destroyed the last traces
Of vanquish'd Macbeth
Built his own castle
Victoriously on the mount

The castle that stands at Inverness today
Was built in the 1830's
A majestic impression of
Red sandstone sovereignty
With a statue of Flora MacDonald
To grace its entrance way

Perched overlooking the city
The river flowing serenely
Below
A footbridge takes you across
From side to picturesque side

One of the most livable cities in
Scotland, they say

Inverness

Even the name is magical!

THE DEATH OF KINGS

Old Duncan was killed in battle, Bill
Not in the dramatic cushion of a horrible
Night's unfitful sleep
The Porter screaming in alarum

No, Macbeth not quite so cold
In the real glare of gone yesterday

But, oh, you gave him blood
The sludge of ambition catching
In his veins
And great conjecture to finger his wife
Old Gruoch
Lost like a ripped-out page

Of history

These things we see now in our minds
Immortal
The truth long hidden in shades unworthy
To take the pen of poets
Who glean 'neath the covers this daily bed
The radiant sun of morrow.

THE PAINTED PEOPLE

Mysterious, shadowy
Enigmatic

The people of eastern and
Northern Scotland

The Picts

Naked warriors
Tattooed and covered in
Paint from head to
Foot

Terrifying
In battle

They left no written records
Their language - long
Forgotten

Who were they?

All that remains
Are some curious
Symbols carved in
Stone
And some beautiful
Objects of
Art

Were they so different
From those who express
Themselves in art
Today?

The tattoos of
Personal identity
That tell us who we are
And where we've been

In the end
All we can say is
The Picts
Are a part of us

They are still here.

THE DRUID'S SPELL

Powers grow stronger
In the rising fires of year upon year
A witches' brew of words
Taking flight in hob-gob fantasy

O the spirit conjured
Soars
Far beyond this earthly veil

Mastering at last
The cunning depths of gargoyled nature

Hail! You harbingers of the Great Dark
Mystery

The night enraptured by the day
Seize the wand from these gnarled fingers
Cast your spell in the ancient tongue

This is the rite, avaunt the wrong
The flesh falling
The dream revealed

A sparkle of dust to sweep the floor.

ORKNEY:
THE WAKE OF THE DRAGON'S HEAD

The islands of Orkney
Will take you way, way, way
Back in time

A Viking ship's journey through

Mesolithic
Neolithic
Pict and
Old Norse
Settlements

Skara Brae is older
Than Stonehenge or
The Great Pyramids
So well preserved
It's called the
"Scottish Pompeii"

70 islands make up
The Archipelago
The largest is called
The Mainland

(You wonder who came up with that
  brilliant name)

The locals are known as
Orcadians
And have their own particular
Dialect:

Part Norwegian
Part Scottish

Visit the Ring of Brodgar
On the Mainland

The Knap of Howar
On Papa Westray

Or the Midhowe Broch on the
West coast of Rousay

Nothing is of the ordinary
Out of body abandon abounds
White sandy shores
Clear blue water
Wildlife
Museums, arts and crafts
Watersports
Hiking and biking

A Viking adventure awaits

All you have to do is
Dip your oar in the water.

THE LOCH NESS MONSTER

What is it that we look for?
What are we hunting in the depths of our
Murkiest seas?
What is it that we need to discover?
What is it that we need to believe?

Will the mystery solved give us some
Solace or peace?

Or is it the mystery itself that
Captivates us and makes our lives
Somehow more dramatic and more
Meaningful?

The Loch is beautiful enough
With or without a Nessie
Isn't it?

And Castle Urquhart
Is a wonder in itself
Scuttled back and forth
Between the Scots and the English
In the Wars of Scottish Independence

Still, we demand more from the loch
We demand a myth and a legend
And a shaft of moonlight we can stick
In our pocket and take home

There are monsters waiting for all of us
In the pitch black voids of our
Most secret desires

Until we can grapple with the beast
Without apology, full front
In the bold light of day
The hunt will continue and the mystery
Of swirling waters and
Silent bubbling ripples

Will endure.

EPIPHANY ON THE A87

How refreshing
Miles and miles
We travel along this road
And not a single billboard
A single commercial
Assaulting our senses
Selling us some inanity
And desecrating the
Beauty
Of this entrancing
Landscape

Everything is in color
The natural color of tree
And bush and flower
And sky
Loch by secret loch...

Guess what, Toto?!
We're not in America anymore!

EILEAN DONAN

The most iconic of Scottish
Castles

A brave sentinel standing guard
Over the guid land of
Kintail

Commanding a stretch of island
Where three great sea lochs
Meet
Loch Duich, Loch Long and Loch Alsh
In the Western Highlands

Founded in the 13th century
A stronghold of Clan Mackenzie and
Their bodyguard allies of Clan Macrae

Destroyed in the Jacobite Rising
Of 1719
Left in ruins for almost 200 years

Purchased in 1911
Painstakingly restored by
Lt. Col. John MacRae-Gilstrap and
Finally re-opened in 1932

Now a national treasure
Thanks to the vision of one man

Without these few determined
Individuals
There wouldn't be much left of the
Past for any of us
To enjoy

All peoples and all cultures
Should take note

Life is much more
Than the evanescent present

We should do all we can
To preserve our antiquities

Lest we forget who we are.

THE HIGHLAND CLEARANCES

The Great of my great great great grandparents fled
The bonnie shores of Scotland
Pinched for a penny by unscrupulous lairds
The time the land was cleared
A human no match for a breeding sheep.

Herded to a boat on a forbidding sea
The fatal winds to blow them—
Some would succeed and others would die—
To America, Canada and
Far-off New Zealand.

They made their way as best they could
New lives planted in a stranger's field
Looking forward, not glancing back
Suns rising, moons falling
Every day a possibility

But there will always be the lingering cry
The broken song of the Highlands
To be forced away
From the home you love
The place of your belonging.

GETTING AWAY FROM IT ALL

While eating the best veggie pizza
Ever
At a little café
In Broadford on Skye

A woman at the next table
Politely asked,
"Where are you from?"

"Portland, Oregon,"
We replied.

To which she said,
"Oh, I'm from Texas."

The man at the table
In front of us said,
"I'm from San Diego!"

And the woman
Two tables over said,
"I'm from Seattle!"

We came to Scotland
To meet Scots
And all around us –
Americans!

So we turned to the
Waitress and asked,
"What part of Scotland
Are you from?"

"I'm from New Zealand,"
She said
With a smile.

Portree Awakening

On a rainy morning
Full of portended
Gloom
What could be more
Delightful
Than little schoolchildren
Crossing the thoroughfare

Like the Beatles
On Abbey Road

See them skip across
In their bright
Red slickers
Hand in hand
Buddy to buddy
From one safe sidewalk
To the other

Their teachers giving
Guidance and direction
Watching with careful
Concern
The beaming yellow
Macks on their backs
Shining like beacons of love

There is something
Inviolable here
Universal and true
Kindness passed
In the simplest of acts

From one generation
To another

Peace will come to the
World this way

Some more eloquent than I
Have said:

"And in the end
The love you take
Is equal to the love
You make"

If only we would
Let it be.

Duntulm Castle

On the north coast of Trotternish
Clinging with its last breath on
The Isle of Skye
Hangs Duntulm Castle
The 17th century seat of the
Clan chiefs of the MacDonalds of
Sleat

What it must have been
In its time
We can only guess
Now there are but a few
Crumbling walls

Of stone

Legend says
One terrible night
A nursemaid holding the infant heir
Playfully in her arms
Lost her charge, by accident
The babe tumbling from
The towering height of the
Window
To the jagged rocks below

As punishment she was cast
Adrift
In a small boat
On the North Atlantic
Left to the vagaries of the sea
And certain death

Such tales give us glimpses
Into another time
Beyond our reckoning
The people who inhabited
This forlorn shore
The competing elements of
Earth, wind, fire and water

And human inadequacy on the
Precipitous edge of
Survival.

Museum of Island Life

Let's not kid ourselves
Most of our ancestors
Were simple people

Ordinary people
Decent people, too

On Skye, you can discover
What their lives
Were really like

The crofter's life

Stone cold cottages
With thatched roofs
And hard earth floors

Fires burning peat
On open hearths

A mattress filled with straw
For a bed

And every home
Had a bagpipe, a fiddle
Or a bodhran
Music and imagination
To lift
Their spirits

You might think it would be
A hard life
Not having
Stuff
To pass
The time

But what they had was
One another
They had stories
They had friends
They had families
They had love
And they had laughter

And what do we have now
In this 21st century
With all our technology
Our gadgetry fixed
In front of our faces
Until we can no longer
See
Our own reflection in the
Mirror?

Hard as their lives were
And as easy as ours are now
Who's to say
Whose life was better?

We don't know, do we?
Or do we?

What myths do we tell ourselves
Now
That prevent us from finding
The truth?

SKYE LOST

There is a thought that comes to me
On Skye
As the wind whips through the heather
Swaying on the purple hillside
Peaks of long knowing
Cloaked in the mists of time lost days

I try to hold on, to keep what is evident
In mind
But the drift of the place is old
And the uselessness of trying to be
Present gives way to a solitude that
Isn't of this time and place

Something takes hold of me
Steals my breath
Carries it out to sea
Every last piece of myself
Broken
Collected somewhere
Perhaps
On some fantastical shore

Perhaps

Perhaps then
If I can find it
I can find myself
But for this moment
I am gone
I am nothing

I never was

And nothing matters
Not even me.

THE ORNSAY LIGHTHOUSE

Thomas Stevenson
A lighthouse engineer
The father of the novelist
Robert Louis Stevenson
Built the lighthouse on
Eilean Sionnach
Isle Ornsay
In 1857

It's an alluring muse
To contemplate

Perched on a crust of rock
East of Sleat, off the Isle of
Skye

The Hills of Knoydart
Offer backdrop
And majesty
To its intermittent
Proclamations
Of light

Oft painted and photographed
The shifting moods
Of sea and sky
Are beguilingly captured and
Recreated
Over and over again

In the artists'
Evocative
Imaginations.

MID-CHEW

What is it that the ram sees
Looking at me

Human walking by
To stop and stare

For an instant

The grass grows
For the eating

The sheep fattened
For the slaughter?

Not for me, thanks
I prefer to

See the sheep
As part of the landscape

A brother made
For this beautiful place

With just as much right
To be here as I

More perhaps, for
I am the intruder here

I will leave you to your
Business, brother

I am honored
That you have allowed me

To share this fleeting pastoral
Moment

With you.

Armadale Castle

The Home of Clan Donald

Flora MacDonald was married here
In 1750
Johnson and Boswell visited
In 1773

In 1925, the MacDonalds
Moved to a smaller house
Leaving Armadale to the
Wind and rain

Photographs show
As late as 1965
It was still a glorious place

A main hall
Lavishly furnished with a
Drawing room off
To one side
And a billiard room
Off to another

A staircase at the far
End
Leading to a suite of
Bedrooms and a
Library

But what was once
So magnificent

Is today but a shell
Of its former self

In so short a time
What was vibrant
And full of life
Becomes but a sigh

That ever so discreetly
Slips like a phantom
Into that last fading wisp of
Twilight.

The Museum of the Isles
Clan Donald, Skye

Step into the gallery and step into
Another world

Like a cave lit by firelight

You can see
The longboats coming
The Vikings on their way
Druids weave their spells
Casting shadows on the walls
Stonehenge giants greet
The sun, the moon and
The stars

The ancient Bards are singing:

"O Children of Conn of the
Hundred Battles
Now is the time for you
To win recognition.

O sturdy heroes
O most sprightly lions
O battle-loving warriors
O brave, heroic firebrands..."

O Children of Conn remember...

Somerled, the progenitor
The Lordship of the Isles

"In ther time was great peace and welth
In the isles thro the ministration of justice"

Peace, wealth and justice

Elusive qualities, these three
We still seek
To know
Their meaning

Across the centuries
The tales
Of a clan
Of a people
Are written in the minds
And in the hearts
Of those who wish
To know

Go on the quest
To the netherworlds
Find your answers
And find
Yourself.

FERRY TO LOCHABER

Sometimes the unexpected
Journey
Is as good or better
Than the hoped for
Arrival at a distant
Destination

The Caledonian MacBrayne
From Armadale to Mallaig
Made the going
From beautiful Skye
A sad parting to be sure
Memorable and pleasant

A full Scottish breakfast
Cooked with care by
Our Gaelic hostess
At 14 Camus Cross B&B
Put us on our way to
The ferryboat landing

A ticket to the taker, then
Driving aboard
The car parked in its
Vagabond space
We headed upstairs to the
Passenger deck

The sun rising boldly
Without obstruction
Sparkled on the water
Like a treasure chest of
Diamonds
Scattered across the wave

The peaks of Knoydart
Were hiding in the gray
Ghost-like haze
Of morning
As we cast off from our
Mooring

Bands of golden light
Streamed through the windows
Spilling
In kaleidoscope patterns
On the dining tables
Where we kicked back

To relax

Armadale Castle bid us
Farewell
Calling from the shore
Getting smaller and smaller
As the vessel made its way
On its 30-minute sail

The bow of the boat
Outside on the deck
Offered a blast of spray
And cold, fresh air
Full in the face and
Through the hair

Gripping
A cup of coffee
Freshly brewed and
Steaming hot
Kept the hands warm
All the while

As we looked around
There was
On the face of each fellow
Passenger
The hint of a smile
An unmistakable

Inner contentment

Such moments
Are rare
But necessary
We collect them as we may
Take them in and
Cherish them

Too short, too soon
The journey ends
Packing up our responsibilities
We, denizens of the world, head
Back down the stairs
Into our cars

Start our engines

And off we go...

THE LIGHT OF IONA

"That man is little to be envied
Whose patriotism would not gain force
Upon the plains of Marathon
Or whose piety would not grow warmer
Amid the ruins of Iona."
Samuel Johnson, English poet and essayist

A tiny island
Off the southwest coast
Of Mull
In the Inner Hebrides

Scotland's cradle of Christianity

In 563, Columba landed
And began his missionary work
The desolate island transformed into
A bastion of learning
Contemplation and
Healing

Poetry flourished on this diminutive
Fragment of earth

The monastery library became one of the
Greatest
In Western Europe
A tremendous light in a very
Dark age

The Book of Kells
One of the most resplendent works of
Art
Ever created
Doubtless had its origins here

Pilgrims from many lands
Made the journey
To this holy place

Many of the long dead kings of
Dalriada
Scotland and Ireland
Norway and France
Were laid to rest in its sacred ground
The Relig Odhráin:
Kenneth MacAlpin
Duncan I
Macbeth
Donalbane

St. Oran's Chapel
Within the graveyard
Dates to the 12th century
Perhaps
Built by Somerled himself
The Lord of the Isles

You cannot help but feel
The magnitude of the ages
The lives that have come and gone
Seeking
Sanctification and
Reconnection to the
Infinite.

OBAN

It's hard to find a more
Picturesque town than
Oban

The Gateway to the Isles

Set like a jewel on the
Firth of Lorn
Near the mountains of Morvern
And Ardgour

McCaig's Tower
Above the town
Looks like a miniature
Colosseum

Close by the shore is
Dunollie Castle
Stronghold of the MacDougalls

Of course, there's a distillery here
And many a place else in
Scotland
A wee dram
Never too far away

Gaelic is the culture
And the ancient tongue
By many
Is still spoken

You might learn Gaelic, too
If you linger for awhile

Especially after a wee dram.

INVITING INVERARAY

Where can you go
To visit a castle
And actually meet the Duke
Who lives there?

Inveraray

The ancestral home of the
Campbells
The Dukes of Argyll
On the West Coast of
Scotland

Quite remarkable that
In the 21st century
You can find the Duke
And his family
Catering to the needs of
The guests who regularly
Visit the castle

And a splendid castle it is, too!

Torquhil is the present Duke's name
The 13th Duke
Son of Ian, the 12th Duke and his wife
Iona Colquhoun of Luss

There aren't many clans
That have so effectively preserved
Their ancestral heritage
Across the centuries of history

But the Campbells have managed the feat
Quite well

If you're a Campbell in any branch
Of your family tree
You simply must go

Inveraray is calling
Connect with your clan
Roots

The Duke and Duchess
Are ready to receive you
And welcome you once again
To the seat of your ancestral home.

Harry Potter's Jacobite Steam Train

Is that you, Harry?
Taking the train to Hogwarts?

The steam billowing from the smokestack of
The Jacobite
Expressly intended
From Ben Nevis to Mallaig

I see you running
Steel tracks clicking
Steady and true
Ft. William to Glenfinnan
The beginning of the '45
Prince Chairley
Raising his standard
On the shores of Loch Shiel

21 arches on the viaduct
Bridge us to a place of
Dreams
Wonderful memories and
Fanciful places made real
In our imaginations

I'll meet you there, Harry
At Hogwarts
I have a trick or two up my sleeve
That you might find

Interesting.

CALEDONIAN MAD CAR DISEASE

Driving on the wrong side of the road
Left not right
Dodge the sheep
Steer clear of the cow
Little tiny wee dee wee dee
Unpaved road
Ka-thunk!
Watch out!
Where's the nearest   .
Passing place!

How long does it take
To get the hang of it
Anyway?

Stick shifting used to be
So easy, but now
The grind of gear to gear
Is unnerving
Especially
In the middle of a

Roundabout

Going round and round
And round and round
Missing the exit
Round and round
Time after time
Where's the sign
And what does it
Mean?

I thought I spoke
English
But now I'm not
So sure
Oh no!
Don't tell me!
The roads aren't marked!

Whoa!
Don't get hit by the bus!
Whew!
Same to you, pal!

Befuddled and
Befrustrated
My heart stuck
Midway between
My sanity and
A Nightmare on Elm Street
I pull over at the
Nearest opportunity

To catch my breath
And collect the wits
I scattered all over
The inside of the car!

Next time it's a Sat Nav
And an automatic
Or else I'll just stay
Home.

The Piper at Glencoe

Glencoe in sunlight
Is glorious
Green treeless hills and
Rocky crags

A piper stands in his MacDonald
Kilt
Plays a lament that reverberates
Through the glen

Tourists with their cameras
Click and smile
A tour bus spewing fumes
The story getting lost

In the 21st century

The piper knows
Though the sun shines bright
Many a lost soul lingers
In these forgotten passes

If you listen closely
You can hear the screams
Of women and children
And frail, old men

One terrible night
Death and destruction

Kind and giving hosts betrayed
A government turned

On its people

It was not a Campbell-MacDonald dispute
As many would have you
Believe
It was about a king demanding obedience

There is many a lesson to be learned
But so few seem willing to consider
In a world that turns its back on
History.

How could anyone with a heart
Commit such vile atrocities
And live with himself in the
Morning?

When does a soldier, duty-bound
Disobey an immoral order
At risk of his own personal
Advancement?

When does a people hold its
Government accountable?

When does love and honor and
Respect of all human beings

Supersede the petty, mean and
Violent ambitions of

A selfish, closed-fisted few?

Glencoe holds the answers perhaps
Trapped in the glen, trying to escape
The piper listens to the cries
And plays

If you look closely
You can see it in his face

The piper knows.

LUSS ON LOCH LOMOND

The A82
Weaves its way down
The western bank
Of Loch Lomond
Skirting by the shore
A matter of feet no more
Glimpses of the glassy blue
Loch
Permeate the trees
Sunlight catching
On green leaves
Dancing

This is no time to be
Missing the moment
Rushing by as
The busy world calls
Unnecessarily

A stop for a rest
Is a must
In the luxurious lap of
Luss, Argyll and Bute
Home of the Clan Colquhoun

Take the time
To stroll the lanes
The model village
Built for the workers
In the 19th century's
Sawmill and cotton mill

Peek in the windows
Of the bagpipe works
The kiltmaker and
The general store

Folks by the busload
Catch the ferry
To Rowardennen
The West Highland Way
Awaiting
Ben Lomond visible
In the north

We sit with a paper bag lunch
By the Luss Parish Church
Christianity brought here
1500 years ago
By Saint Kessog
Who was said to make miracles

Taking in the view
You'll think so too
A blessing is bestowed
On all weary travelers

Take my advice
Take the High Road or
Take the Low Road
But get there
Be it soon or
In your own good time

But don't wait too long
The things that distract
The things that you think matter
Really don't

Trust me.

THE GOVERNOR OF DUMBARTON

Lost on the way to Dumbarton Castle
Left turned into a petrol station
To get some directions
To put us back on track

The cashier couldn't be bothered
But the stock boy heard our pleas
And waved us over

Did I say stock boy?
No, this was no stock boy
Though that may have been
The job in which he was stuck

No, this guy was Erik the Red
Flowing hair
With the Viking look of Thor
In his eyes
Intellect sharp
As the blade of an axe
And the nicest
Bloke you could ever hope
To meet

Spent a good twenty minutes
Showing us maps
And detailing the
Back and forth
Options on the
Lay of the land
Traffic light here
Traffic light there

One last left
And straight on till morning

When we said goodbye
To his pearly white teeth
We felt we'd met a brother
For life

Dumbarton was grand
No question about it
But the lad in the petrol shop
Was even grander!

GLASGOW SUNRISE

Watch the sun emerging through
The dusky skies of Glasgow
Carefully and with
Reverence

The working heart of Scotland
Beating to its own pulse
Situated on the River Clyde
One of the largest seaports
In Britain

The Scottish Enlightenment
Took hold here in the 18th century
Great minds considered how
Reasonable human beings
Could create a world for
The betterment of all

The University of Glasgow
Founded in 1451
Is still among the finest in the world
For Arts and Sciences
Law, Engineering, Medicine

The hard working men and women
Who make Glasgow their home
Come from the deepest roots
Of all that it means to be
Scottish

Their ancestors have inhabited
This land

For thousands and thousands
And thousands
Of years

They will not be stepped on
And spit out
By those who would exploit them
For less than honorable
Ends

They are called upon now
In this 21st century
To find a way
To bring health and prosperity
To an ailing world
Being consumed in the fires of its own

Delusional

Greed

Glaswegians keep their eyes
Focused
On what is honest and true
What is good for the old
And good for the young
The weak and the poor
What is fair
What is decent

And what is cruel

Enlightenment
Education
Hard work
Compassion
Truth

These are not words
To be taken lightly
When Glasgow speaks

The world must take notice.

AN AYRSHIRE FARM

I thought I saw
Robert there kneeling
In the muddy sod of an
Ayrshire Farm

A horse bending over
To nibble a bit of hay

A bucket on its side turned
In fury
Somehow knocked over
By a swift kick

In the ribs

There were words
That found their way
Through the poet's hands

There were thoughts
That were forbidden
In the Calvinist clutch
Of sobriety

The days might have seemed
Foolishly wasted
The landlord's cracks
Too bitter to embrace

All would come their way
In the short winding of a
Lifetime

All would be forgiven
In the substance
Of a dream

The soft curve
Of an eyelash
And a kiss that waits
Upon the lips

These would bring
The foundering heart to its
Fruition

These would steady
The hand
That gripped the pen

And pulled the reins.

ST. BRIDE'S KIRK
5 p.m. on the deserted streets of
Douglas, South Lanarkshire

The iron gate was ajar
We pushed it open and went in
A graveyard filled with giant
Tombstones
Centuries old

The grass was soft
Beneath our feet
Slightly muddy
From a not long ago
Drizzle of rain

The old church was
Partly in ruin
The clock on its tower
Said to be the oldest working
Clock in Scotland
A gift from Mary, Queen of Scots

This was the final resting place of the
Mighty Douglas family
Who ruled this land in ancient times

My wife said she heard voices
Coming from inside the church
We went to the door and
Knocked
But no one answered
The voices were silent
And the door was locked

A sign instructed the curious traveler
To contact the Key Keeper
For entrance

In an apartment building not
Far away
We found an old grandmother
Her grandson playing in the yard
She nodded as if she were
Expecting us
Withdrew into the building
And when she returned
She placed a huge iron key
Into the palm of my hand

Empowered
I heeded the call of my ancestors
Went straight to the Kirk door
A solid block of worldly wood
Inserted the key upside down
To unlock the mystery

The key turned well enough
And we could hear the lock unlock
But pushing the door
It refused to open
Turning the key this way and that
Pushing and pounding but nothing
Would budge
Exasperated, I was about to give up

But my wife would not relent
She was a McDonald, after all
With one more determined push
The strength of Somerled
Surging through her arms, her legs
And the uppermost thrust of her body
She blew
That door open
A blast of old air came forth
Struck her in the face
Knocked her out of the present
And into the past
An experience she will never
Forget

We entered
An old holy shrine
To the dead

Dark and forbidding, yet
Serene
Watched over by a beautiful
Stained glass window
Rendering a soft, peaceful light
To the tombs etched into
The walls

There lay the effigies of
James "The Gross" 7th Earl of Douglas
Resting for eternity
Next to his wife, Beatrix de Sinclair
He died in 1443

A privilege for me and my wife
To see them here reposing
Together
Almost 600 years later

Nearby was James's nephew
Archibald, the 5th Earl of Douglas
Son of Archibald, the 4th Earl
Whose wife Margaret Stewart was
The daughter of King Robert III of
Scotland

The 5th Earl's sons, William and David
Only 16 and 14 years old
Were murdered ceremoniously
At the Black Bull's Dinner
In Edinburgh Castle
Their wealth and lineage too much of a threat
To James II and his powerful advisors

But the tomb I came most to see
Was the grandfather of them all
The Good Sir James of Douglas
Also called "The Black"
The Right Hand Man of
Robert the Bruce
Brothers in Arms
At Bannockburn

He died in battle
Fighting the Moors on
Crusade

Whilst returning the heart of The Bruce
To the Holy Land
Fulfilling the request of his dying
Friend

What remains of the Good Sir James
Lies here in this
Beautiful chapel
His stony leg broke off
His face but a smooth blur
Of worn stone
And his heart in its own coffin
Imbedded in the floor

My warm hand touches his cold effigial form
With gratitude

Ancestry is a hard thing
To wrap your mind around
When you go this far back
In time
We all come from such places as
This
And someday, if we're lucky
We might return
To pay our respects

Consciousness is in many ways
A matter of choice
We choose what we wish to know
What we wish to experience

What we look for
And what we hope to find

Whatever adventure we choose
It always delivers in its promise
Of knowing ourselves and our
Fellow travelers on this tiny blue
Planet Earth
Just a little bit better
And leaves us
Upon reflection
With just a little more
Wisdom.

Oh yes
And what about those voices
My wife heard inside the church?

What was that all about?

Some things have no explanation
And remain forever
A mystery.

One Morning in Laurieston
Dumfries and Galloway

The mist covered the curve of country roads
And the tops of trees and hillsides
An airy drizzle that seemed to caress
The first light of day
Breaking through the clouds
And bend it slightly to the welcoming
Kiss
Of an eager traveler

A single intersection marked the
Place where white washed
Houses lined the way of the quiet village
Known as Laurieston

Tucked serenely in the
Back pocket of an out of mind
Industrial world
Those quite forgotten
Byways of Kirkcudbrightshire
Dumfries and Galloway

Scotland

There was a time
Long, long ago
When they called this place
Clachanpluck
Clachan meaning village
Pluck being the center

The center village, then
Of Balmaghie Parish
Bordered by the River Dee
To the north and to the east

Dark Times there were then
Dark Times indeed

The red kite flying high above
In watchful waiting for unwary
Prey

This was the homeland
You see, we think
Of some ancient McDonald
Ancestor
Who in the dark age known as
The Killing Time - 1685
Fled this place, fearing for his
Life, perhaps
Or the lives of his unfortunate
Friends
Religion and belief too dangerous
For the politically powerful but
Intolerant

On a quick masted ship
He embarked
And made his way
To America

His daughter of many generations
Hence
Crossing that ocean once again
Lands on sodden ground
And windswept pavement
Here in Laurieston
Breathes the dew-laden scent
Of birch tree lanes
And lightly puddled sidewalks
Flowers opening in front yard
Garden beds to greet
The wayward passer-by

She tries to capture
In her mind
A glimpse of a man she
Will never know
A ghost who wanders
Elusively
In and out of buildings
That were and might have been

Is he smiling now?
She wonders
He with his grand fathers and grand
Mothers
Now that she, the very first of his
Descendant line
Has returned
Returned home
To the place
Of beginning?

She is smiling sure
The streets may not recognize her
They may not see her flowing red hair
Or the Sleat gray twinkle of her eye
But she knows now
She knows she belongs

At the edge of the road
Beside the last house
Of this scarcely populated
Tiny clachan pluck
The end of her long journey
She kneels by a stone cairn of a monument
Proudly set on a lonely
Hillock

The plaque
Bears testimony to the poet
Samuel Rutherford Crockett
The native son who
Gave voice to this place
Novelist and tale weaver
On the worldwide stage

He spoke of a hamlet
Called Pluckamin
Not far from this place
Close by it was said
The Bargatton Farm

It was he whose words
After all
Resonated across the sea
And led her here

Pluckamin
A place that is no more
A place no longer remembered
Here, in Scotland
You won't find it on a map
But the place still lives
Namesaked with an "e"
In America, in New Jersey

From Pluckemin to Pluckamin
New Jersey to Scotland
She has come
She has returned
From 2014 to 1685
Over three hundred years
She has traveled
And the memory still lives
This place is not forgotten
It is home
Once again
And will always be.

COFFEE IN KIRKCUDBRIGHT

The best places to go
Are the places
Off the beaten track
The places the tourists
Don't know about

The unsung places
You won't find in the books
Like unsung people
Without pretense
Without show

They're real places
Like Kirkcudbright
Or
Ker KOO bree
As the locals say

An artist's town
In the Stewartry
Of Dumfries and Galloway
At the mouth of the
River Dee

Life flows like the
River here
Calmly
Into the waiting waters
Of the Solway Firth

White, red, yellow
Flowers

Line the way
As you amble down the
Main street

The buildings painted
In green, blue, purple
And peach pastels
A baker's goods appealing
To your sense of smell

Boats and crews
Are busy at the wharf
A working harbour
That gives this place
A certain charm

The old ruin of MacLellan's
Castle
Dating back to 1577
Presides with a flair of mystery
Over the scene

John Paul Jones was once
Held prisoner
In the old Tolbooth
Now a gallery for the local
Artists' inspirations

We stop in a café
Chat with the owner

Sip the hometown brew
From a table on the
Street

Old folks passing
Mothers with their strollers
Children with their dogs
Greeting one another
As they go by

A small town simplicity
Seems harder and harder
To find sometimes
No worry
No hurry

Relax.
Unwind.
Enjoy.

THREAVE CASTLE

It takes a while to get there
But that's part of the adventure
You have to walk through
Many a farmer's field
Along a narrow path
Fenced in
From gate to gate

The surrounding countryside
Leaves itself wide open to
Your gaze
Take in the scent of the fertile
Soil, the green grasses playing in the wind
Along the rolling hills
Of Balmaghie

At last you will see it
A massive stone structure
Straight and tall
Rising out of the landscape
Bold and defiant
Like a sentry
Demanding
"Who goes there!"

Built by Archibald the Grim
Third Earl of Douglas
Towards the end of the 1300's
On the site of a fortress previously
Owned by Alan, Lord of Galloway
A century before

In 1451, William, 8th Earl of Douglas
Kept a retinue of a thousand men
Armed for war

In 1455, King James II
Brought siege and
According to legend
Sent a blast from Mons Meg
Smashing through the castle wall
Taking the hand off Margaret Douglas
As she raised her glass to drink

The Douglas' power was beaten down
And the castle passed to the Maxwells.

The keep is situated on an
Island
You must ring the bell
To alert the ferryman
For crossing
The fork of the River Dee

You the genealogist
Might say your ancestors
Were Douglases and once owned
This castle
To which the ferryman will reply
"Great! I've got some unpaid bills
For ye then."

Standing next to it
You look up

Five storeys high
If your imagination is apt
You might see the archers
Crouching at the windows

Inside
The dungeons
The kitchens
The great hall
The loo
These were people, too

A raging fire to keep them warm
A well to quench their thirst

Power is an elusive thing
Temporary, fleeting
And so much blood is spilled

Hundreds of years slip by
From one lord to another
Peasants baking bread

And no one now, no one
Remembers, or even cares

Ring the bell
The ferry's waiting
To take you back
To your own disgruntled
Time and place

We are continually
Dissatisfied
Creatures, aren't we?
Life never quite what we want
Or desire
And in the end, what have we got?

A ruin of stone
That strangers might visit
But if they learn something
In the cracks of the pieces
Of themselves
Well then
Perhaps
That is, in itself
A worthy gift.

DOWN IN DUMFRIES

"I hate this town," he says.
Young college-age lad
Selling cell phones in Dumfries.

"I may be a tourist, but
For God's sake, son," I says.
"This was the home of Robert Burns."

"He's dead," he says.

"Not to me, he's not," says I.
(Starting to get into my Scottish pirate's voice)

"Look around ye, lad. Don't be blin'.
There's guid-ness aawhaur. Aye, that
There be. And guid-ness in aabodie, tooo."

(My brogue was just starting to
Catch fire)

"Just look at me an' look at ye.
What's the difference, I ask ye.
Shuir, I got a fake Scottish brogue
(That sounds a little bit Irish)
An' ye got the real one
But as Rabbic said,
A man's a man for a' that."

"An a' that an a' that," he says.

"That's right," says I. "If ye ever
Forget who ye are or what life's
A' about, just look to Rabbie Burns.
Right here in Dumfries. He walked
These streets. This was his toon!
That's somethin' to be
Prood of.
This is a sacred place, m' friend."

"Robert the Bruce was hereawa! Don't ye forgit it!"

"Me. I'm just an old mouse. A wee
Sleekit' cow'rin tim'rous beastie.
My time's almost up, but ye?
Ye have the whole warld
Afore ye."

"Don't just stand here quarrelin.'
If you haate your job,
Get another one.
If you hinna got a girlfriend
Finnd one.
If your life's a bore,
It's likely to be your own
Bluidy fault!"

"It's do or dee, laddie.
It's do or dee!"

MURDER IN THE CHURCH

The Bruce called the meeting
In 1306

At Greyfriars Kirk
In Dumfries

The Kirk as a holy place
Would be a place of safety

Or so it was thought

The future of Scotland
At stake

The Red Comyn arrived
And words were exchanged

But what really happened
No one knows

Except that Comyn
Lay dead on the floor

History is often like that
Many a tale is spun

To justify one side or
Another

The victors usually
Get their way

And it goes down thusly
In the history books

But you, as a seeker of truth
Must look deeper

For me, it is personal
The Bruce was my ancestor

But strange as it may seem
The Comyn was too

You see, that far back in time
If you're lucky on your quest

You'll find your ancestors
Your kinsmen and your cousins

On both sides of the conflict

At Stirling Bridge
At Bannockburn
Culloden and
Flodden

Your grandfathers be
Both English and Scots

And Welsh and Cornish and
Irish, too

So how can you root for one
And not the many other?

The Bruce emerged from the Kirk
That day, and the Comyn lay still and

Silent

There's a truth somewhere that
Still remains hidden

But it's up to us to find it.

LADY DEVORGILLA'S BRIDGE

Lady Devorgilla of Galloway
Daughter of Alan, Lord of Galloway
And mother of King John Balliol
Toom Tabard

He who became the puppet of
England's Edward I

Her mother, Margaret, was the niece of
William the Lion
A great granddaughter of King David I

When Devorgilla's husband, Sir John
5th Baron Balliol died in 1269
Lady D had his heart embalmed
She kept it in an ivory casket
Bound with silver

One of the most powerful women
Of her day
She founded Balliol College, Oxford
Built New Abbey and
The convent of Greyfriars in Dumfries
Where The Bruce murdered
John "The Red" Comyn, Lord of Badenoch
Her grandson
In 1306

The bridge over the River Nith
Still bears her name

She died in 1290, aged 80

On her instructions
She was buried
With her husband's heart beside her
In New Abbey

Such was her enduring love

The monks renamed it
Sweetheart Abbey
In her honor
Though over the years
The graves
Of the lovers
Were subsequently
Lost

Time in ruin around them.

BURNS HOUSE
Dumfries

How many countries
Would you guess
Have a poet
As their national hero?

Burns epitomizes
The humanity
Humor
And egalitarianism
Of Scotland

Entering his house
You get a feel for the man
Who he really was
Simple in his tastes
Honest
True
Not at all materialistic
Or pretentious

His humble desk and chair
Were probably amongst his most
Prized possessions

There is a window pane
Upstairs
From which he oft
Must have gazed
That bears his signature
Carved into the glass

What was he thinking on that day?

Did he see mortality
Beckoning from afar?

At least the glass
Would remember
He was there
Centuries and
Centuries
Hence

Burns died here in 1796
When he was only 37

There is something sad
And sacred
About walking quietly
From room to room and
Seeing his bed
Feeling the loss of a man
Taken away
Much too soon

But what he gave the world
And particularly Scotland
Will never be forgotten

At least as long as
Humankind
Is capable of dreaming
Of better worlds
And kinder people.

Universal Brotherhood

Going to the Bank of Scotland
For some ready cash
Delighted to find
Robert the Bruce and
Robert Burns
Commemorated
On the face of the
Bills

When I returned to England
I still had some of those
Scottish pounds
In my pocket

Went into a convenience
Store for some bananas
And nuts

But when I tried to pay
With my Scottish notes
The clerk refused them

"We don't take those."
He said sharply.

Taken aback, I said,
"Why not?"

"My boss won't let me
Accept them."

He smiled, as if to say,
"There's nothing I can do
About it."

I may not be a Scot
But let me tell you
I was deeply offended

It's against the law
To refuse to accept this
Legitimate currency

If you want to know why
There's still bad blood
Between the English and
The Scots
Just look in the mirror

All of you

Take a good long look

And you will find your answer.

THE YES AND NO CAMPAIGN

My heart says Yes
My head says No

Which is wiser?
The head or the heart?

When your gut tells you to do something
Do you listen?

Or do you doubt yourself,
Do you give in
To fear?
Fear of the unknown.

Do you go back and forth
Inside your head
Wondering what will happen
If you do or you don't?

Locked in a vicious circle of
Endless confusion?

Change isn't easy
It's easiest to do nothing and
Suffer the consequences
Painful as they may be.

The unknown will never be known
Until you have the courage
To go through the door.

Do you have faith in the goodness
Of your fellow human beings?

Do you have faith in their intelligence
Their ingenuity and their compassion?

Do you think that they can find a way
To make things better
No matter how great the challenges?

Are you willing to do your part?

There were others who left Scotland
Century upon century
Making their perilous way to a
New and possibly better world

A world they had to create
Themselves.

They said Yes to the challenge
Yes even to the risk of their own lives
And the lives of all of their descendants.

Was it the head or the heart
Or both?

Or neither?

Was it simply determination and
Belief in themselves?

Then again
There were those who
Remained behind
To create a new Scotland

Enlightened and progressive
A leader in science, industry, education
The like of which the world
Has seldom seen.

Yes or No is always the question.

Wisdom is finding the path that is
Best for all
Considering the options, the positives
And the negatives

And having the courage to change
What must be changed
For the sake of the
Entire world.

THE BURNS WHO CROSSED THE OCEAN

Ah cousin, Robert, I hear ye now
In the vaunted hills of my Highland heart
The songs of your sure keeping

Too long away from the mooring
My journey tides the ocean
An epic for the bard

I cannot beg to know my kin
Or speak that ancient tongue
But I do listen, and I do hear

And I can feel in the pass of soul
The kindred tie that binds us
Give me your hand upon the breeze, Rabbie

Time drifting like a feather
Though far away, and far apart
We'll rest our dreams in Scotland's arms

And play our songs together.

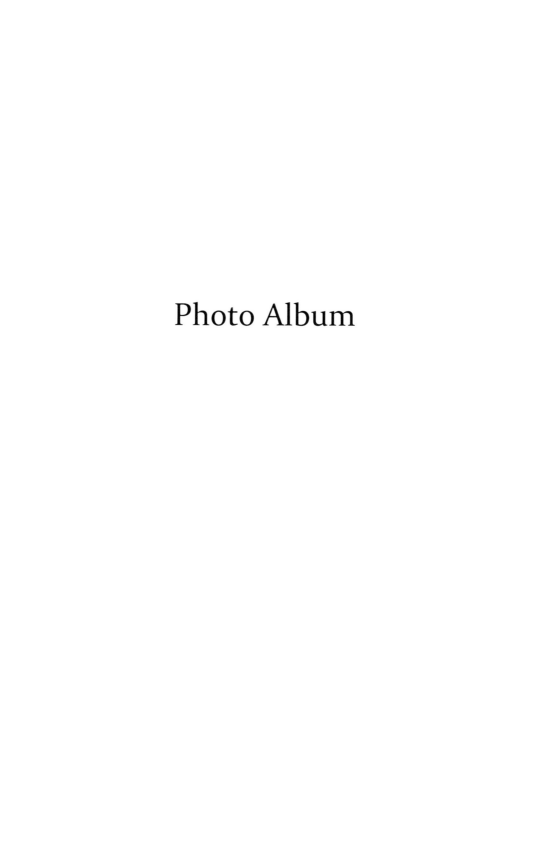

Photo Album

The Unicorn Chained ornamenting the roof of the Great Hall, Stirling Castle

Mons Meg at Edinburgh Castle

The Clan Chief musters his troops (author at center with musket)
Culloden Visitor Centre

Laurence Overmire and Nancy McDonald at Leanach Cottage, Culloden
photo by Ginny Barry, 2014

Schoolchildren crossing the road in Portree on Skye

The ruins of Duntulm Castle, Trotternish Peninsula, Skye

The Weaver's House, Museum of Island Life

The ram, mid-chew, on Isleornsay

Armadale Castle *(above)*,
and the Museum of the Isles,
at Clan Donald Centre, Skye

In ther time was great peace and welth in the isles thro the ministration of justice

St. Bride's Kirk *(above)*

The author entering *(left)*

With effigy of Sir James "The Black" Douglas *(below)*

169

Laurieston, Dumfries and Galloway *(left above)* and the Samuel Rutherford Crockett Memorial *(above right)*

St. Cuthbert Street in Kirkcudbright, with MacLellan's Castle *(upper right of photo)*

Threave Castle, stronghold of the Black Douglases

In Dumfries

Statue of Robert Burns
(right)

Lady Devorgilla's Bridge
(below)

Robert Burns in a
Dumfries shop window

Liner Notes

LINER NOTES

Poetry is as much music as it is language. It is impossible to separate the two. The language creates a music all its own. The experience of reading a book of poetry, then, is perhaps more akin to listening to a record album than it is to reading a book. You have to allow the words and images to move through you and awaken whatever is sleeping within. Be touched. Be moved. Feel what it is to be alive.

Some of the best musicians are poets and vice versa. Think of John Lennon and Paul McCartney, Bob Dylan, Joan Baez, Joni Mitchell, Paul Simon, John Denver, Neil Diamond, Bruce Springsteen, Leonard Cohen, Emmylou Harris, Billy Joel, Elton John, Enya, Steve McDonald, John Legend, Prince Ea and Adele just to name a few. They are great musicians, but they are also insightful poets with important ideas to express.

Poets, too, intentionally create music in the choices of their words: Shakespeare, Homer, Rumi, Lord Byron, Dylan Thomas, Samuel Taylor Coleridge, Emily Dickinson, William Wordsworth, Walt Whitman, John O'Donohue, Maya Angelou, T. S. Eliot, e.e. cummings, Edgar Allen Poe, William Butler Yeats, Edna St. Vincent Millay, Henry Wadsworth Longfellow, Pablo Neruda, Langston Hughes, Sylvia Plath, Seamus Heaney, Mary Oliver, Billy Collins and, of course, Robert Burns. The list of the greats goes on and on and each has his or her own particular style of music. All of them have touched me in some way and wielded their influence upon my own life and work.

These liner notes are offered, as on a record album, to enhance the poetic experience, to provide a little more background for the poems in question.

The Ghost of Rabbie Burns (p.9) is a tribute to my grandmother, Anna Mary Shriver Fast (the daughter of Mary Isabelle Burns Shriver), who chose to marry my grandfather, Irl Fast, a man who valued learning, education and basic human decency. My grandmother represents my deep personal connection to the poetry of Robert Burns and to Scotland itself. And for that I am deeply grateful. By the way, unbeknownst to Irl, who thought he was primarily of German ancestry, he was also descended from clans Matthews, Colquhoun and Thomson in Scotland.

The Bards of Scotland, Ireland and Wales (p.14) is a lament. The Celtic Bards were the intellectual leaders and truth tellers of their day – the keepers of the ancient stories and traditions, the voice and the conscience of the people. I was reminded of this fact by two ministers, Very Rev. John Macdonald and Rev. John Lincoln, who were part of a team translating the Bible into everyday Gaelic. My wife Nancy and I met them in a charming Bed and Breakfast on Isleornsay on Skye. I hadn't fully realized it before, but I am an inheritor of the Bardic mantle and tradition. As a genealogist, I carry the family stories within me, generation upon generation. As a poet, I choose to be a voice of conscience and reason and an advocate for peace. But whereas the bards of old were highly respected, high status members of the clan, today's poets are misunderstood, marginalized "dreamers" to whom most people pay no heed whatsoever - a sad commentary on our times, perhaps?

The Train to Edinburgh (p.16) marks the beginning of our journey to Scotland. Leaving from London, we were hoping to strike up a conversation with some locals, but the two business travelers that sat across from us were immersed on their laptops the whole time and not much amenable to pleasant conversation. They got off at Newcastle and two Scottish teenagers took their place, so engrossed in the passion of their obviously brand-new romantic relationship that they didn't even notice the two old Americans sitting across from them twiddling their thumbs. Thinking back on that couple now, it occurs to us the lad looked a lot like a 16-year-old Robert Burns. We couldn't understand a word he said, his accent was so thick. Stepping off that train at Waverley Station, my foot landing for the first time on Scottish ground, was indeed momentous for me. My wife Nancy had visited Scotland years before in the eighties. She was delighted to return.

Walking Through St. Giles (p.19). Nancy's immigrant McDonald ancestor came to America, we believe, during the Killing Time of 1684-1685 when the Scottish Covenanters were being persecuted by the English kings, Charles II and James II. St. Giles' Cathedral took us straight back to that time period. We were in the presence of three key figures of that turbulent era: John Knox, Archibald Campbell (1st Marquess of Argyll) and James Graham (1st Marquess of Montrose). There is something pleasantly reassuring to find those bitter 17th century animosities are now laid to rest in our modern more enlightened age.

Greyfriars Kirk and Bobby (p.22). It was said that Archibald Campbell, 9th Earl of Argyll, and his brother, Lord Neil Campbell, were buried at Greyfriars. We searched all over, but we couldn't find them and the docents didn't seem to know anything about it. Bobby, the famous Skye Terrier, is the star attraction at Greyfriars. Dogs are such powerful teachers and healers, aren't they? I think of my own dog, Nicky, my childhood best friend. All these years later, I still miss him and love him dearly.

Proclaim It From the Mountaintops (p.26) is an homage to The Proclaimers, one of our favorite Scottish bands, and *Sunshine on Leith* is one of our favorite songs. As we gazed down from the heights of the Edinburgh Castle walls we were thrilled to notice that there was a narrow strip of sunlight on Leith. Of course, we immediately thought of the song and it played through my head the rest of the day. You know how that goes. In many ways, the Proclaimers accompanied us on our journey through Scotland. We had their music programmed into our iPod, so that we could play some of their tunes as we drove. In Dumfries, we attended a YES rally that we happened upon in the village square. They led everyone in a stirring and heartfelt rendition of *500 Miles*. It was a very joyful and uplifting experience. Thank God for the musicians of this world who bring such happiness, depth and meaning to our everyday lives.

St. Margaret's Chapel, Edinburgh Castle (p.28). Years ago, I discovered that I was descended from King Malcolm III Canmore and his wife Margaret Aetheling, so Margaret is one of my grandmothers, a remarkably caring person in a brutal period of human history. For years and years, I've wanted to visit the chapel and see it in person. It was much smaller than I anticipated and very humble. The chapel itself is believed to have been built by David I, Margaret's son, also my ancestor. When you trace your genealogy, you find connections to many of the people and events that shaped history. History is not the story of some old irrelevant strangers. No. History is your story. Your family was there – your grandmothers and grandfathers, uncles and aunts, cousins, nephews and nieces. If not for them, you wouldn't even be here.

Black Bull's Dinner (p.30). Like I said, all of history is very personal. Those two boys that were murdered – William and David Douglas – were my first cousins, 19 times removed. Their grandfather, Archibald 4th Earl Douglas, was my 20th great grandfather. He was killed on Aug. 17 (my birthday), in 1424, at the Battle of Verneuil in France. The infamous dinner took place in David's Tower in 1440, now part of a truly haunting exhibit at Edinburgh Castle.

Where Wizards are Born (p.32). Of course, my wife Nancy and I are *Harry Potter* fans, aren't you? We had to visit the Elephant House restaurant in Edinburgh where J. K. Rowling wrote much of the first book of her series. There's nothing at all fancy about it. Struggling writers (as most of us are) have to find places that are reasonably inexpensive and won't kick you out if you spend too much time there writing. The window in the back part of the restaurant that overlooks Edinburgh Castle is a must-see. Just down the street from the restaurant is Greyfriars Kirk and graveyard. Reportedly, Ms. Rowling frequented the grounds for inspiration. Indeed, among the gravestones you can find Thomas Riddell, William McGonagall, and Elizabeth Moodie, names which figure prominently in the fictional wizard's world.

Stirling Bridge, 11 Sept. 1297 (p.36). The date of Sept. 11, of course, sends shock waves through every American's heart remembering the attack on the World Trade towers in 2001. William Wallace's stunning victory at Stirling Bridge must have sent a similar terrifying shock wave through the heart of King Edward I of England. He was not about to be bested by this Scottish upstart. He was determined to crush him and, in a few short years, he did.

The Battle of Falkirk, 22 July 1298 (p.37). The most tragic thing about William Wallace is that he was the victim of politics. The people rallied to his cause, but most of the nobility refused to support him. The Red Comyn's role is a mystery. Why did he leave the field? Was he betraying Wallace or did he have legitimate reasons for saving his men to fight another day? In any case, the feeling of betrayal is a common one all around the world as people without wealth and power are abused and exploited by those who should know better.

De Bohun and De Brus at Bannockburn, 23 June 1314 (p.40). We felt privileged to be visiting the battlefield 700 years after the event. The sun shone brightly making for a dramatically beautiful green landscape. It was hard to imagine it could have been the scene of so much bloodshed. Of course, being the genealogist, I was very aware of my family history and the ancestors who fought on this stretch of ground. They were on both sides of the conflict and several of them died here. In fact, if you are able to trace your ancestry going far back in time, you will find it is not at all unusual to find your grandfathers fighting on both sides of most every conflict in the distant past. The realization might even make you pause and wonder at the absurdity of it all.

The Last to Die, Flodden Field, 1513 (p.43). James IV is reportedly my 15th great grandfather through my immigrant ancestor, Samuel Calhoun, who came to America sometime before 1750 and settled in Cumberland County, Pennsylvania. Of course, going this far back in time, you have to take these reported ancestries with a grain of salt. As at Bannockburn, many of my ancestors were killed in the battle including Patrick Buchanan, George Seton, Henry Sinclair, Sir William Graham,

Sir Matthew Stuart, and Sir John Somerville. By repeating their names here, I honor their memory. I can feel some sense of Scotland's immense loss. Of course, if I had never investigated my genealogy, I would know none of this, the names wouldn't mean a thing to me, and like most everyone else, I probably wouldn't care. Now that I do know, however, the Battle of Flodden is very personal indeed and my heart breaks when I think of it.

Argyll's Lodging (p.50) is situated just down the hill from Stirling Castle. Archibald's brother was Lord Neil Campbell. After the failure of the Monmouth Rebellion and the execution of his brother, Neil knew his own life was in peril, so he quickly purchased land in East New Jersey in America and fled Scotland with a shipload of persecuted Presbyterian Covenanters and other supporters. We believe my wife Nancy's immigrant McDonald ancestor was among them. We were surprised to find that we were the only ones visiting Argyll's Lodging at the time. The docent let us look all around at our leisure, a thrilling experience for us.

The Twa Queens of Buchlyvie (p.53). Our research revealed that Nancy's immigrant McDonald ancestor, whom we have yet to positively identify, may have been one Daniel McDonald of Buchlyvie, a Covenanter. We made the journey to this small village in Stirlingshire just to get a sense of the place. We're glad we did. What are the odds you meet someone in Scotland whose relative lives just down the road from you in Oregon in the United States?

Blairgowrie Hospitality (p.55). It's amazing how people from all over the world can now connect on the Internet. To our complete surprise, we discovered that our Blairgowrie hostess Dianne Brown's mother was a

McDonald. Her family actually lived at the famous Leanach Cottage on the Culloden Battlefield at one time. At the end of our Scotland sojourn, upon our return to England, another Facebook friend, Sally Clarke (a fellow poet) and her husband, Brian, treated us to a delicious dinner near Windsor Castle in England. These very special relationships would not have been possible before the computer age!

Aberdeen City and Shire (p.58). In 1734, my 5th great grandfather, William Scott, came to America. He was said to be from Urie, Aberdeenshire, Scotland. He married Margaret Calhoun of County Tyrone, Ireland, and settled in Pennsylvania near the Susquehanna River. My 20th great grandfather, Sir William Keith, Great Marshal of Scotland, built Dunnottar Castle.

Never Enough Time (p.60). There are many places in Scotland my wife and I simply didn't have time to visit. Many of them we have visited vicariously through research online. Thanks to the Internet it is now possible to get a good sense of other places without having to leave your home, but there is nothing like actually experiencing the place for yourself in real time with real people.

The Clan Chief (p.62). Nancy and I met our friend Ginny Barry from Portland, Oregon, at Culloden. She was touring Scotland at the same time we were. I had investigated her genealogy previously and discovered that she was a descendant of the Keith family of Aberdeenshire. She spent much of her time reconnecting with her ancestral home. The genealogy also revealed that Ginny shared common ancestors with Nancy, and common ancestors with me, albeit many generations back. So we were cognizant of the fact that we were not only friends, but as it so happens, family. The museum and exhibits at Culloden were excellent. I will never forget the chap who recreated the role of the Clan Chief and put me through the paces as his tacksman.

Culloden Moor, 16 Apr 1746 (p.66). I wrote this poem many years ago. I am proud to say it was recited on the Culloden Battlefield as part of a memorial service there on Apr. 17, 2010, though unfortunately, I was unable to attend at the time. It was very gratifying for me to experience the cold, desolate battlefield for myself in 2014.

When Flora Opened the Door (p.68). This was another poem written years before my visit to Scotland. It is certainly steeped in the myth of the '45 Rising, but the historical Flora paid a price for her compassionate attention to Bonnie Prince Charlie and aiding in his escape following the disastrous Battle of Culloden. She was imprisoned in the Tower of London for a time. The Bonnie Prince, unfortunately, did not manage to escape with his dignity intact. The rest of his life was a shiftless blur. He drank himself to a sad and bitter end in Rome, Italy. The myths we tell ourselves it seems, long after the fact, are so much more pleasant and reassuring than the disturbing realities.

The Death of Kings (p.71). William Shakespeare specialized in the telling of "sad stories of the death of kings." History tells us quite different stories. My wife and I felt the Scottish Play reverberating through our heads as we wove our way into Scotland's ancient past, especially as our journey wended its way past Culloden and Inverness, knowing that Cawdor Castle was just to the east of us. *Macbeth,* the play, has a unique power all its own and tells us truths that we could never access through a mere retelling of dry historical fact. Yes, King Duncan was actually killed in battle, not murdered by Macbeth. The historical Macbeth was actually a pretty good guy, relatively speaking. But without Shakespeare's poetic vision, no one would even know or care who these historical figures really were. Nevertheless, in our search for truth we should be able to distinguish fact from fiction and learn from the lessons of both.

The Painted People (p.72). People often ask what happened to the Picts? No doubt they were integrated with the other peoples of the north, particularly the Gaels and the Norse. They are still a part of our genetic heritage. I am reminded of the Picts every day as tattoos have become extremely popular in America. It is not at all uncommon to see people covered in them. They are expressions of personal identity and history, very much akin to the Picts and other aboriginal cultures.

The Druid's Spell (p.74). Age seems to bring out the Druid in me. Words carry incredible power. Hopefully, with a little bit of wisdom we will use that power to do good in the world and right the wrongs that have persisted for ages and ages.

The Museum of Island Life (p.89) perhaps better than anywhere else helps you to understand how truly difficult it must have been to survive on Skye. We have our romantic fantasies about the MacDonalds and other Highland clans, but life was brutish and cruel. Relationships with family and friends were of the utmost importance. Music, poetry and storytelling, in fact all of the arts, must have played a crucial role in lifting spirits during very dark times.

Mid-Chew (p.96) is a true story about my encounter with a ram minding his own business, but checking me out in his leisurely way as I was strolling down a dirt road in Isleornsay. Every creature has a right to be on this Earth. Who am I to disrupt the natural order? "Respect" is a good word worth handing down to our children.

Armadale Castle (p.98) invokes a deep sadness in me. Indeed all these ruined castles do, wishing I could somehow be privy to the grandeur of their former glory. Previous generations either did not understand how precious their history would be, or lacked the means to preserve these treasures. It is a lesson for us all to make the very best of our own time and place.

Caledonian Mad Car Disease (p.114). Both my wife and I are in complete agreement on this: driving through Scotland was sheer hell. It took us 2 hours to escape from Edinburgh. Our Google maps were completely useless. Roads were blocked at every turn. Even now, I'm haunted by roundabouts in my dreams!

The Piper at Glencoe (p.116). I had to play the Ballad of Glen Coe on our iPod as we made our way to this fated place: "O cruel is the snow that sweeps Glen Coe and covers the grave o' Donald." My Tifft ancestors on my paternal grandmother's side were from Glencoe, Minnesota, named after Glen Coe, Scotland. So the name itself carries weighted significance for my family. The story of the massacre is a haunting one. One can't help feel for the plight of the victims. The soldiers, too, must have suffered mightily at the mercy of their own consciences, having to obey the despicable orders of their superiors.

Luss on Loch Lomond (p.119). Luss, on the western shore of Loch Lomond, was the ancestral home of my Colquhoun (Calhoun) ancestors. Across the lake on the eastern side was the home of my Buchanan ancestors. So Loch Lomond figures quite prominently in my own Scottish history. *The Bonnie Banks of Loch Lomond* has always been a favorite song of mine, perhaps in part for ancestral reasons of which I am not conscious. I can tell you I had such a feeling of peace and contentment there on my brief visit. It did indeed feel like coming home.

The Governor of Dumbarton (p.122). Lord Neil Campbell, the brother of the 9th Earl of Argyll, was at one time Governor of Dumbarton Castle. Of course, we had to pay the old castle a visit. As usual, unable to find adequate signage, we got lost. The helpful man in the petrol shop made everything all right. Ordinary people and small kindnesses really make life a pleasure, don't they?

St. Bride's Kirk, Douglas, South Lanarkshire (p.129), was, for me, like a pilgrimage to the Holy Land. This was the home of my Douglas ancestors. Sir James "The Black" was my 21st great grandfather. Touching his cold stone was the completion of a journey I began when I first discovered my ancient Douglas roots in the family tree. It was a deeply moving experience for me to pay my respects.

One Morning in Laurieston, Dumfries and Galloway (p.135). We believe my wife's McDonald ancestor may have come from the vicinity of Laurieston. We met a friendly local on his way to work after buying a loaf of fresh-baked bread. We told him the story of our quest to find the McDonald ancestor. He said the historian Ted Cowan lived nearby and suggested we go see him. That sounded well and good, but where did he live? Which house? He didn't provide us with that information. He went on his way. We started down a lane to search out Prof. Cowan, but the loud rantings of an angry Scotsman and a barking dog not far away convinced us to change our minds. We now regret we didn't make more of an effort to find the historian. Whether or not he would have appreciated meeting us early in the morning unannounced and uninvited, who knows?

Threave Castle (p.143) was built by Archibald "The Grim" Douglas, the son of Sir James "The Black" Douglas. Archibald was my 20th great grandfather. His son, Archibald 4th Earl Douglas, my 19th great grandfather, was killed on my birthday in 1424 at the Battle of Verneuil in France. Shakespeare immortalized the 4th Earl in *Henry IV, part 1*. He was defeated by Hotspur Percy at the Battle of Homildon Hill in 1402. One of the most amazing things about our visit to Threave was that very few people were there. We had the whole place almost entirely to ourselves, albeit there were two four-year-olds running through the ruins with plastic swords in their hands, doing battle as they went. They "captured" their mothers and put them in the "dungeon." "How long do we have to stay here?" one mother implored with a smile on her lips. The boy thought for a moment and exclaimed, "Two hours!" A fitting punishment for an impertinent mother in need of a time out.

Down in Dumfries (p.147). I often try out my fake Scots accent in the comfort of my own home in West Linn, Oregon, but I dare not use it in public and certainly not in Scotland. In the secret fantasy of a poem, however, I rather enjoy the sound and sheer audacity of it and rapidly become an expert of all things Scottish in my own foolishly American mind.

Murder in the Church (p.149). A truly heinous crime. John "The Red" Comyn, Lord of Badenoch, by the way, was the same man who sided with William Wallace, but withdrew with his cavalry from the field at Falkirk. The Red Comyn was my 23rd great grandfather. Robert the Bruce was my 21st great grandfather, so you won't find me siding with one man over the other here. What happened in that church was a fateful and criminal act, no matter who was largely responsible. But don't miss the point of this poem: they are your grandfathers, too, whether you are aware of it or not. As a genealogist, I have seen the Big Picture as very few have. Most people now living have no clue who they are and where they come from. We are all descended from the ancient kings of our various cultures. There is nothing unique about it. And let's be honest, most of those kings were pretty ruthless individuals. What's important for us today is that we wake up to the fact that we are all literally cousins. How would our world change if we honored that relationship and started treating one another as family?

Lady Devorgilla's Bridge (p.152) in Dumfries reminds us of the important role women played in the Middle Ages. Some, like Lady Devorgilla of Galloway, wielded a great power for good. When we were there, a YES rally was marching across the bridge. We met some of the leaders of the rally, who were women. They expressed deep concerns about social issues and the suffering of their families, friends and neighbors because of misguided political policies. As it turned out, Dumfries and Galloway and the Scottish Borders all came out strongly against independence with a NO vote.

Universal Brotherhood (p.157). While most of our major religions acknowledge the truth of universal brotherhood, too many human beings are still hanging on to their hate and fear of "the other." We have created our own misery. We can also heal ourselves through kindness, cooperation, compassion, generosity, forgiveness, honesty, understanding and sacrifice. The choice is ours.

The Yes and No Campaign (p.159). The Yes or No vote for an independent Scotland took place on Sept. 18, 2014, the day we were flying back to America. Scotland voted No 55.3% to 44.7%. We were not terribly surprised after talking to Scots all over Scotland, many of whom were fearful of leaving the Union. As outsiders listening to the news broadcasts and debates, our feeling was that there wasn't a strong enough vision for what an independent Scotland would look like. As Americans of Scottish descent, we definitely felt the romantic pull of Scottish independence and an innermost part of ourselves yearned for it. As a genealogist, I also knew that among my ancestors were not only Scots, but also English, Welsh, Irish and Cornish. I have an affection for the entirety of the UK and its people. So, for me, choosing one side over another is kind of like saying one side of my family is more important than another. The political truth that we all should acknowledge, however, is that the status quo in many countries, including the United States, is not working for a great many people. We have to find a sustainable way of living, especially in the face of serious challenges like climate change and wealth inequality. The selfish and greedy interests of an elite and powerful few, manifested in huge multinational corporations and financial conglomerates, have taken precedence over the needs and interests of people and the planet. There will be change. There must be. Will it be for better or worse? We must decide. Hopefully, wisdom will guide us. Personally, I would like to see Scotland become a more forceful leader for clean, renewable energy and sustainable living, as well as a global advocate for enlightened thinking, ethical business practices, higher education and equal rights for all people. I am confident that Scotland can be such a force whether it is ultimately independent or remains a vital, contributing partner of a United Kingdom. In any case, Scotland cannot do it alone. The UK cannot do it alone. All good people all over the world will need to work together, summoning our courage and the best parts of ourselves to lead the way to a prosperous and healthy future. Doing the right thing, surrendering our short-term self-interest to serve the needs of the whole, has never been easy for humankind, but now, more than ever, that is exactly what we must do. Future generations are counting on us.

The Burns Who Crossed the Ocean (p.162) is a poem I wrote many years ago. It has a much deeper significance now. I have embraced Robert Burns and his beloved Scotland. I have heard the music of the authentic mother tongue. I have walked where he walked, lived where he lived if only for a brief time, and seen where he died and where he was finally laid to rest. The ghost of Rabbie Burns will continue to walk beside me. And when I am gone, I will walk beside others who fight for the cause of truth. The truth is love. No I will never be a Scot, but I have a new awareness of what it is to be Scottish. My forebears played a significant part in making me who I am. I honor their legacy. I will never forget what they gave me. I will love them until the day I die. And no one can take them away from me.

ABOUT THE AUTHOR

Laurence Overmire has had a multi-faceted career as poet, actor, director, educator, genealogist and public speaker. As an actor, he appeared on Broadway in *Amadeus* directed by Sir Peter Hall, as well as the television soap operas *All My Children* and *Loving*. He was also executive producer of The Writer's Lab in Hollywood, a non-profit organization to promote quality writing in the entertainment industry.

Overmire's poetry has been widely published in the U.S. and abroad in hundreds of magazines, journals, and anthologies. *The Ghost of Rabbie Burns* is his fourth collection of poems.

The author at Burns House, Dumfries

Overmire is also the author of four epic books of family history. Having spent much of the last two decades immersed in genealogical and historical research, he has created several genealogical reference databases on the Internet including *The Ancestry of Overmire, Tifft, Richardson, Bradford, Reed*, which has received over 1.8 million hits and has helped hundreds of thousands of people trace their family trees and find their connections to famous historical figures.

The book that has drawn the most worldwide attention, however, is a philosophical work titled, *The One Idea That Saves The World: A Call to Conscience and A Call to Action*. Overmire calls it "a blueprint for world peace."

It has been widely acclaimed for its compassionate, common sense approach to many of the world's most pressing issues.

Overmire is very active as an advocate for peace, social justice and the environment. He was one of the contributors to *Global Chorus: 365 Voices for the Future (2014)*, a collection of essays by some of the leading thinkers and humanitarians of our age including Dr. Jane Goodall, Archbishop Desmond Tutu, Nelson Mandela, The Dalai Lama, Bill McKibben, Jamie Oliver, Alexandra Cousteau, Dr. David Suzuki, Wendell Berry, Stephen Hawking, Maya Angelou and Paul Hawken.

Very concerned about the health of the planet, Overmire is a proud signatory on the International Declaration on the Future of the Arctic, joining Sir Paul McCartney, Emma Thompson, George Monbiot, Naomi Klein, Prof. James Hansen, and many others, to call for effective measures to preserve the Arctic for future generations.

"We need to stand up, protect and defend the things we love," Overmire says, "but we need to do so with understanding and compassion for all."

He lives in West Linn, Oregon, with his wife Nancy McDonald.

For more about the author, see *laurenceovermire.com*.

Lightning Source UK Ltd.
Milton Keynes UK
UKOW02f0715080516

273739UK00001B/39/P